Livi_ _ volume 1

Ed. *Rib Davis*
The Lightbox

Woking Living Words, Volume 1

© 2007 the Lightbox

Printed by Biddles Ltd.

ISBN 978-0-9555166-0-3

Front cover photograph:
Martin Bowman

Rear cover photographs:
Carnival Float, 1930s
Woking News and Mail
Carnival Float, 1990s
Martin Bowman

My father-in-law took on this smallholding in Moor Lane to grow 'Shoesmith's famous chrysanthemums'.

Editor
Rib Davis

Chapter Editors
Jill Bowman, Gill Cossey, Alison Craze,
Rib Davis, Marion Edwards, Caroline Self,
Jean Simpson, Elaine Slatter, Ray Ward

Administrative Assistants
Jill Bowman, Emily Craze, Sarah Giles

Photography Editors
Peter Hall, Victoria Nisbett

Photograph Researchers
Jim Chisholm, Richard Christophers,
Rosemary Christophers

Design
REG Design

Interviewers
Hilary Alder, Nicola Bleasby, Sarah Brown,
Bridget Conigliaro, Margot Craig, Alison
Craze, Amanda Devonshire, Barbara Fisher,
Kathy Garratt, Rib Davis, Ann Harington,
Miss K Higgens, Janet Hill, Julie Jacks,
Aparna Jugran, Valerie Keary, Jan Mihell,
Ann Monaghan, Olivia Richards, John
Sayers, Emma Seward, Marilyn Scott,
Katherine Sharpe, Jean Simpson,
Mr Steer (jnr), Zoë Thomas, Margaret
Waters, Ray Ward, Mary Walters and
students at Bishop David Brown School,
St John the Baptist School, St Mary's
School, Byfleet and Byfleet Primary School

**Transcribers, transcript checkers
and proof-readers**
Rita Barron, Irene Boston, Jill Bowman,
Martin Bowman, Sarah Brown,
Richard Christophers, Rosemary
Christophers, Bridget Conigliaro, Gill
Cossey, Margot Craig, Alison Craze,
Quentin Cross, Jim Chisholm, Rita Davies,
Marion Edwards, Diana Farndale, Steve
Flinn; Karen Green, Ann Harington, Tony
Kelly, Pat Lambert, Jo Lee, Jan Mihell,
Pearly Palmer, Caroline Self, Jean Simpson,
Elaine Slatter, Chris Smeeton, Maureen
Thomas, Zoë Thomas, Ray Ward, Gill
Washington, Anne Wolstencroft

**The Lightbox is also particularly
grateful for the co-operation and
support received from the following
individuals and organisations:**
Bishop David Brown School, Tony Brittain,
Byfleet Primary School, Tony Charters,
Colin Chivers, Trevor Dean, Keith Goodale,
Francis Frith Archive, Mike King, The
Maybury Centre, James McCarraher, John
Scott Morgan, Mohammed Ilyas Raja,
Mufti Liaquat Ali, Reuters, David Robinson,
Mrs J. Rozelaar, Sheerwater and Maybury
Living Words Project, St John the Baptist
School, St Mary's Primary School, the
Shah Jehan Mosque, Brian Skinner, Surrey
Advertiser, Surrey and Hampshire Canal
Society, Surrey History Centre, Unwins,
James Walker, G White, Woking Asian
Women's Association, Woking College,
Woking History Society, Woking Local
History Forum, Woking News and Mail,
Woking Photographic Society.

**Woking Living Words gratefully
acknowledges financial support
from the Heritage Lottery Fund.**

**The Lightbox gratefully acknowledges
financial support from Woking
Borough Council.**

Contents

I met my husband at the Atalanta Ballroom in Woking and quite a few people met their husbands at the Atalanta Ballroom.

History is too often seen as something dusty from the past, but in fact we have all lived our own histories, and lived our communal history, and it is that living history which this book celebrates.

Foreword

Over my lifetime Woking really has changed almost out of recognition. Of course the Common is still there, where my brother Eric and I first put bat to ball, and some of the older streets still remain, but much of the town has been utterly transformed. The way we lead our lives, too, has altered enormously. Childhood, for my generation, was not a matter of computer games, tv shows and fast food. The games were active, the amusements we made for ourselves and the food was fresh. My brother Eric and I walked to school every day one and half miles there and back at the age of five – wonderful exercise.

I am delighted to endorse this publication, which traces those changes in the words of the people of Woking. History is too often seen as something dusty from the past, but in fact we have all lived our own histories, and lived our communal history, and it is that living history which this book celebrates. Some of the changes I have seen have been for the better; some, I believe, for the worse. Here they are recorded, through the voices of those who lived through them, for the interest – and at times, perhaps, amazement – of readers both present and future.

Sir Alec Bedser
Woking, September 2006

Introduction

Views of Woking vary greatly. Some find it a very pleasant place to live, with beautiful commons and woodlands close by, a vibrant centre, affordable housing and convenient transport links. Others find it a boring, even tedious place. In Douglas Adams' mock dictionary *The Meaning of Liff* (sic), 'woking' is the word for going to the kitchen and then not remembering why you went. A certain Richard Rutter has written, 'Most people pass through Woking on the train from London to Portsmouth. I wouldn't recommend you stop, as Woking is dull, dull, dull.'

Is Woking really dull? It actually has a fascinating – and very unusual – history. Old Woking is an ancient settlement, but Woking itself only sprang into life with the arrival of the railway in 1838. In the short period since then it has grown into a major town, with a multi-cultural population. Within the borough there are a number of unique landmarks, including the Shah Jehan Mosque (the first purpose-built mosque in Britain) and Brookwood Cemetery, originally intended to accommodate all of London's dead, not to mention the magnificent McLaren Technology Centre and Woking Palace.

And what has it really been like to live here? This book is about the texture of people's lives in this place. It is not a history in the sense of a text book, told with authority and apparent objectivity. No, this is mostly so-called 'ordinary' people talking about their personal experiences, and reflecting upon how their lives here have changed over the years.

This book is about people's lives in this place. It is not a history in the sense of a text book; this is mostly so-called 'ordinary' people talking about their personal experiences, and reflecting upon how their lives here have changed over the years.

I have had the pleasure of leading a group of very able volunteers in making the tape-recorded interviews of hundreds of residents of the borough, from all sorts of backgrounds and ethnicities, for this project. It has been a fascinating process, and one which I think all the participants have enjoyed. This book is one of the results of that process, along with the edited transcripts and sound extracts which are being used in the History Gallery of The Lightbox, in our educational materials and on our website.

The words you will be reading, then, were originally spoken rather than written. Spoken language is, of course, rather different from written language. It is more spontaneous and often less grammatically correct, as well as frequently including hesitations and repetitions. In editing this book we have tried to retain much of the spontaneity of the original spoken words, while at the same time editing out those elements which go un-noticed in speech but would look rather odd on the page. We have also deleted the questions that were asked in the interviews, and on occasions this has led to our adding the odd word or two to make the answers alone comprehensible. These are, however, very small alterations, all done very much within the spirit of the original speeches.

The chapters of this book roughly correspond to exhibition areas within the History Gallery of The Lightbox, though there is no chapter of oral history on Brookwood Cemetery for fairly obvious reasons. The exhibitions on Brookwood Hospital and Mental Health are little represented here either, as we shall be producing another volume of oral history devoted entirely to these topics.

This book cannot possibly touch upon every aspect of life in Woking within living memory. I am aware, too, that some important projects, such as the Ockenden Venture (now Ockenden International) do not receive a mention, as they do not quite fit into the scheme of the book. In future volumes we certainly hope to make good the omissions.

At the back of the book you will find a list of contributors and their years of birth. As our selection has been based on topics rather than chronology, it is sometimes unclear as to the period of an event described; the inclusion of years of birth should go some way towards clarifying this.

I am very grateful to everyone who has been involved in this project. These include the interviewers, transcribers, photographers, transcript checkers and chapter editors. Most of all, of course, I am grateful to all of those – over two hundred people – who agreed to be interviewed. Many of them are represented in this book; the interviews with others may well find their way into future publications.

I believe that Woking Living Words shows that living in Woking has, in fact, been anything but dull.

Rib Davis
March 2007

The only thing is the houses
are very close and, I think,
that's what was strange.
They're close, they're shut
all the way round. In Pakistan
it's open houses.

I grew up actually in British
Army camp in British Far
Eastern Colonies with
Gurkhas. Gurkhas serve
in British Army.

Winston Churchill say, if
you obey English law you
could stop here. I stayed.

1. Coming from Afar

One of the beauties of this
country has been its ability
to accept other cultures
and other religions and
I admire that within the
British people.

I was nearly fourteen when we came to England. It was exciting because we had read about it. We came down on the train, we saw these weird things on the roofs. That was my first impression, all the chimney pots. In Canada and U.S.A. we had gone electric and central heating had dispensed with coal fires. So many of them! Because there were fires in every room then; and smoky, and it was so cold. It was just awful – everything! All the pipes froze because they were all on the outside and that's the way it was and ice on the windows. In Canada we didn't mind the snow but we got warm when we went inside our houses. But here was only a little fireplace in the sitting room, so it was always best to get lit. But you get used to it, you have to I suppose, but the central heating in those days was considered unhealthy and if they had any form of central heating, it was pretty primitive; they always had windows open. Not just one, so you either sat in a howling draught or with frozen feet, it was awfully difficult to get it right.

We stuck out like sore thumbs because they didn't know any foreign person in that school.

My father said the trains to Woking are more frequent and the journey shorter. That's why we moved here. We were house hunting and we got out of the station and saw ladies, very elegant ladies on sit-up-and-beg bicycles, high up bicycles with their three-quarter length voluminous skirt and black stockings and gloves and a hat cycling. Now in North America, the only people who ever went on a bicycle were children, teenagers maybe; workmen also cycled. We were so surprised, that was our first sight, these black stockings, and they all had them. You either had black or flesh coloured lisle which was considered rather below standard.

Only bathing once a week in England, because of heating up the water. That did surprise us.

The house my parents chose, it was possible to put in central heating. It was the plumber's first central heating job for a private house and he had to look up all sorts of things and find out. It was very funny. They put in another bathroom. One bathroom with six bedrooms and nothing else, one toilet for the house and one downstairs but that was normal. So we put in another bathroom and altered little things, Only bathing once a week in England, because of heating up the water; Saturday was bath night. That did surprise us, because we were very bath minded and showers, we loved showers there.

People began to call on my mother and if she was out, they left calling cards with their address. This is 'calling' – this is how neighbours get to know the new arrivals; it's a courtesy in the whole of Britain. They called between 3pm and 4pm. My mother had to return the calls, so she hastily got cards printed. That was done until the War and the War changed everything. We went to St Mary's Hill School, Woking which was called 'a gentlewoman's school.' My mother said, 'What a snobby start!' We stuck out like sore thumbs because they didn't know any foreign person in that school. Nobody travelled far and if they did, it was business or moving. So they were very ignorant and they'd get us at recess, break as they call it over here, and say, 'Now, Katharine, talk Canadian.' We couldn't do anything else! 'What did you do in Canada, did you live in wigwams?' They were so ignorant. The work was arduous because we were decimalised in North America and pounds, shillings, pence and farthings and everything was most bewildering. Miss du Bouchet taught literature, as she called it. We didn't get on very well. Once I said, 'This is a yat.' Miss du Bouchet said, 'That's "yacht" in this country, none of your foreign language.' I said, 'I didn't know that, this is my first day being taught in England.' They were so ignorant about other people.

My parents' friends came and played bridge, but never for a drinks party. Canada had prohibition and that started them I think. Our parents were almost 'tee-total' and were amazed at the hospitable offers of alcoholic drinks, which altered after the War.

Katharine Buchanan

They'd get us at break, and say, 'Now, Katharine, talk Canadian.' We couldn't do anything else! 'What did you do in Canada, did you live in wigwams?' They were so ignorant.

Winston Churchill say, if you obey English law you could stop here. I stayed.

Well, my husband's Polish, his brother lived in Horsell and we thought it would be nicer to be closer to his brother. He came over with the Polish Resettlement Corps in Scotland, where they were being re-trained. Then they were going back to France to fight. Then, because the War ended they were given the opportunity of staying in England and his brother had already settled in Woking. We applied to the Council because we lived with my parents and the house was condemned. It was a very old Victorian house and, after the bombing, it was, virtually, just sinking.

Winston Churchill say, if you obey English law you could stop here. I stayed.
Betty and Karol Heller

We applied to the Council because we lived with my parents and the house was condemned. It was a very old Victorian house and, after the bombing, it was, virtually, just sinking.

Mr Waterer's house was in the nursery, Waterer's Nursery, and Mum used to do the cooking and she used to go back in the evenings and she used to do the dinners for Mr and Mrs Waterer. So we found out that these young chaps who were working in the nursery were all Prisoners of War, and Mr Waterer came down to us one day and he said, 'Oh, Mrs Stevens,' he said, 'You couldn't put a young man up, could you?' he said. 'He's a German boy and he wants somewhere to stay.' And of course I was at home then and I had John and you know Mum and I were sort of struggling – well I was working 'cause Mum was looking after John for me and so Mum talked to me about it. She said, 'Well I wonder if we could have him as a lodger.' So I said, 'Well that's up to you Mum, we got the back room,' 'cause Mum and I used to sleep in a bed in the front, 'cause we only had two bedrooms. I had a little cot for John and we used to sleep together, Mum and I. Well that's what you used to do. So I said, 'Well that sounds all right.' 'I think we will have that young man,' she said, 'come and live with us'. I said, 'Are you sure?' 'Yes', she said, 'but we won't be able to understand him 'cause he speaks German'.

So we managed all right 'cause I mean I got a job and I used to go off and leave Mum and that, you know, and she said, 'Yes, he can sleep in the back room.' And so I met him and it was so funny 'cause we couldn't understand him, you know, he was jabbering away there. I said, 'Mum what's he talking about?' 'I don't know,' she said. Mrs Smith along at the end of Littlewick there, she thought it was horrible that I got friendly with this chappy and that sort of thing, you know, but I never took any notice of them. Eventually we got him talking good English, eventually, Mum and me sort of got him to, you know, and I mean he was wonderful. In the end he fell, I was going to say he fell in love with me, well I suppose he did and also John, young John because John was only a little one.

We went once back to Germany. Oh, it was a lovely place. Do you know I was terrified 'cause you see I'd never been outside of Woking.

He tried to explain it to me that he was quite happy in England and he didn't want to go back. His Mum and Dad were alive but then they died after we got married. Of course I never met them and it was very sad but I said, 'Well it's up to you, if you want to go back home, you go back home,' but he didn't want to go. We couldn't make him go back home. He was quite happy being with us.

We went once back to Germany. Oh, it was a lovely place. Do you know I was terrified 'cause you see I'd never been outside of Woking. I'd never been abroad or anywhere like that and he said, 'Well,' he said, 'What we'll do, we'll save our money and we'll make an effort', he said, 'and I'll take you to see my –' well I couldn't see his parents 'cause they'd died while we were married but he had other cousins and nephews over there and he said, 'That's what we'll do.' 'Oh', I said, 'I'll have to go and get one of these passports things you see and have my photograph taken.' I was terrified 'cause I hadn't been out of the country. I mean I was only a country girl and I'd never been abroad before and there was all this funny language but we had a wonderful time.
Molly Voelkl

I was born in Clapham in London, but I came to Woking when I was about thirteen months. My father was a builder but he'd lost all his money in the '29 crash and found it very difficult in London, and so my grandfather lent him some money to buy the hand laundry in Eve Road. It was called The Alpine Laundry, so we moved there. My earliest memory is sitting in a laundry hamper while my mother worked one of the machines, the pressing machines. We lived there until about 1942.
Barbara Chasemore

Ladies working at Rose Cottage Laundry, 1932. It is said that the parrot was taught some colourful language.
Lyndon Davies

Aerial photo of what was to become Sheerwater estate, 1945
English Heritage. (NMR) RAF Photography

My husband wanted us to move from London. He'd had enough of London. It didn't bother me, I liked London. Just the noise, the hectic life there really. He just wanted to get away to the country. It was just the life itself, it was just too much for him, and he said, 'I want to move out to the country.' And I said, 'If that's what you want, that's what we'll do.' I loved London, so I was happy enough but he's the one that wanted to move.

It was very peaceful. I didn't realise that I would like the peace of the place. You don't, if you lived with a lot of traffic and that.

The shops were lovely. Little old shops. It was very peaceful. I didn't realise that I would like the peace of the place. You don't, if you lived with a lot of traffic and that. You get used to that. I always lived near trains. Seemed to be wherever I moved we had trains at the back so I was used to a lot of noise but I felt I could relax more and, in fact, when I used to go to London, I hated it. Couldn't wait to come back. And the air was so much better. Much clearer air.
Evelyn Cowley

I can remember coming in on the removal van and thinking it was wonderful because it was all new houses. There wasn't a lot. I mean, there wasn't many shops. I can remember that and thinking, 'Where's my mum gonna do her shopping?' Although Raynes Park wasn't very big anyway. But, yes. I thought it was nice.
Janet Hicks

We lived near Blackfriars Bridge, near Waterloo, and my dad always had a little business, we always lived in a café or over a shop. In fact, when we moved to Sheerwater this was the first house that we'd ever lived in. We came down and we viewed here and we couldn't believe it but the one thing about the houses here, once I got used to them, there's one room I love and that was the bathroom and I still do now, I go up in that bathroom and that is where I shut myself away, you know.
Renee Illinesi

L C C Sheerwater estate, 1952
Surrey History Centre

My ancestors down there were all fisher folk – they came from Margate originally, the whole family has hundreds of years in Margate and lifeboat men and fishermen with their own boats. That's why my father's family came up, searching for work I should think in the early 1900s. They lived at Anthony's for a time.
Pamela Green

We lived at SE17 and we moved down because our house was condemned and they moved us down to Woking. My parents, naturally both Londoners; my mum and dad had six children at the time. Then of course we came to Woking.

It was countryside to us. When we came down here and we see the house, it had a gate and a pathway down to the door and it was such fun, because it was snowing at the time and the house was lovely.

Well it was countryside to us. When we came down here and we see the house, it had a gate and a pathway down to the door and it was such fun, because it was snowing at the time and the house was lovely.
Joyce Gee

We had one room. The Council offered us – we could either go to Redhill or Woking – and we decided we'd come to this one.
I was miserable wasn't I? Because we went up to a top flat and it was like being a bird in a cage, I hated it. I had the baby. I didn't have a pram shed, so I was popping up and down all day every day. I needed to get out, used to walk into Woking almost every day. When it was winter, we put a hot water bottle in the bottom of the pram to keep the baby warm, but it was putting the pram up and down the stairs. Now you imagine it, you know, when I think about it now, no wonder I'm going to physio.
Mr and Mrs Bell

When it was winter, we put a hot water bottle in the bottom of the pram to keep the baby warm.

We used to live in a basement flat, a run down typical London flat, you know, rats running around everywhere, so obviously we went in for a transfer and they moved a lot of people from London to Woking for some reason.
Derek Drake

I'm from a village in North West Frontier, near Peshawar city. I lived for a long time in that village. My grandfather used to do business, import export from India for a long time during the British Empire. After my grandfather, my father and my uncle they inherit the business. At first I studied in my village, in the local school. Then I went to move to near the business and I studied. After that I come here and I married my wife here and after that, I settled down here.
Deran Shah

My father was a builder and decorator.
Of course, in those days, if it rained, you
didn't work and if you didn't work there
wasn't any money. So my mother, as with
all the neighbours, used to be waiting outside the pawn shop on a Monday morning
to get some money to feed the children.
Even when she had all us children she used
to get up at the crack of dawn and walk
to the City to office clean and then she'd
walk back and get us all off to school and
so she didn't have really much of a life.

We had a twenty-two room boarding
house in Clapham Road so she also took
in boarders and then the War came so my
mother, being the woman she was – she
was quite a character – she hired a lorry
and we packed in as much as we could on
the back of this lorry and come down to
Woking. She rented two houses in Goldsworth Road. She not only brought my
sisters and my married sister with her children, and my married sister's neighbour,
who begged could they come along, so
we all turned up in Woking on the day the
War was declared. We got down here just
after midnight and that was quite comi-
cal. When we got here, my mother hadn't
got the keys, so we had to break in and
the next thing we knew the police arrived
on the scene because neighbours had said
people were breaking into these empty
houses. I was twelve years old then.
Doris Moles

**I was living in London at my mother-
in-law's house, where we had two
rooms, the wife and I.** The back of the
house was still bomb damaged so we
moved here. The people in Woking didn't
like us very much, they thought we was
'common' coming from London, us 'common people on a council estate.' And
they'd titter about you in the queue, you
know, but they found we were a great ad-
vantage to em 'cause all us going up there
and shopping did them a lot of good.'
William Oldall

The people in Woking didn't like us very much, they thought we was 'common' coming from London, us 'common people on a council estate.'

**Wandsworth Electrical came here
in 1952 escaping from Birmingham,
where it was completely flattened
during the War.** All three factories up
there were made to rubble and in the first
planning permission available after the
War, we came south because there was
no regeneration of building in Birmingham
at the time and we were the first site on
Sheerwater, where there were no houses
and the LCC's agent plonked his wooden
hut on our patch.
Richard Salter

St Dunstan's RC Church, White Rose Lane, 2006. The church was built in 1925
Martin Bowman

Just before the war, my mother got very worried, remembering that the Germans had come over in the First World War and bombed London. We were staying with an aunt in Tolworth on the 1st September and my mother got on a Green Line bus with my young sister and said to the driver, 'Where's a good place to go to get away from the bombs?' and he said, 'Well, what about Woking?' So my mother got off at Woking with my sister and being good Catholics went straight to the St. Dunstan's Church, to the parish priest, and said, 'Is this a good place to live?' and he said, 'It's a very nice place to live and there's a nice Convent here for your two daughters and I know of a house that is about to be let and you could take it and see how you got on.' So that's what my mother did and it was a very big house in Hook Heath and she invited four of her sisters to come with their husbands and children to join her in the house. That's how we started in Woking.
Bernadette Rivett

Footpath to Old Woking, 1908 *The Lightbox*

We had a very nice minister in Fleet at our church and my husband-to-be was the youth leader and I was working in the Sunday School and he considered us clever, useful workers, so when he came to Woking he wanted us. We wanted a place of our own which he found. So we came to see it late at night and she said, 'Oh but there's no lights up there. You must come in the day.' We couldn't do that. So she gave us a torch and we took the flat by torchlight, but it was a very nice big house, with lovely big rooms.
Serena Whiteman

My mother said to the driver, 'Where's a good place to go to get away from the bombs?' and he said, 'Well, what about Woking?'

I don't like to feel too hemmed in and what I really love about Woking, it's such a green place.

We came to this part of the world after a long stay abroad, we came back in the mid-'80s and settled. I suppose you get off a plane and you settle somewhere near Heathrow basically. I don't like to feel too hemmed in and what I really love about Woking, it's such a green place. Such good efforts are made to keep it green and it's just about a good size I think as a small town and of course it's got lots of things we like, like the theatre and so on.
Hilary Mantel

I used to travel around a lot, all over England. Thirteen years ago I moved down here. It was a very hard life. Like it was going to be here today or we might be down a different part of the country. Most time we travelled round Manchester area. Mostly the winter in Manchester. Summer-time we'd go down Devon and Cornwall and different parts of the Midlands. Just around. To every kind of borough and that just for our work.

At that time a lot of the men didn't work so much. It was most of the women. Mostly telling fortunes, selling goods door-to-door. That was most of the thing we used to do at that time.

Most of us who've settled down on sites, most of us are Christian, 'Born Again Christians', so now we don't do no fortune telling and just try and get means and ways to get our living by different things like garden work, tree topping, tarmacking.

Well, most of the time now you can't travel round so much now. Since, I think it's about '91 I think it was, there was a law come out. Gypsies come under it but it was mostly out for the New Age Travellers. Most of the gypsies who travelled about for all our lives, like from generation to generation, were more or less made to be settled down because there was nowhere where we could pull in. If we stopped somewhere we would be there for a day or two days and were moved on. So, it's very difficult to travel about now, especially when you've got kids growing up. We want to get our kids into school and to have a good education because most of the older ones never had much of an education because they don't seem to settle but for us in England. The last twenty years a lot of us are starting to settle down. But, it's got its good and its bad.

I think the funniest thing was when I first went to a house and I couldn't feel the floor hollow underneath me and it was a frightening thing for me. I mean, when I first went up like a stairway, when I was walking up the stairs, I was bending down, getting lower to the floor because it was, like, strange because we've only been, like, in caravans and before that we was in what we called wagons, used with the horses and before that there was tents.
Harry Lee

I was born in Shanghai, China. My actual home village was in Canton. My parents were working in Shanghai. After the War with the Japanese invasion I moved back to my home village with my parents and that was in 1931. I was married at twenty years old. My husband also worked in the village, in the field, a peasant.

Why we decide to move here is because of Tiananmen Square, yes? It's that event. I think it's the massacre.

When I came over here, everything is very, very different. Even in a hospital, of course, the food is so different first of all and we seldom had potato, just boiled potato, never at home, and then the first three years I was so hungry. Because I arrived in November. In those times, the weather was so dull, really almost black every day and it's so cold.

My first impression in Britain was I find the British people are friendly. When I went out on the streets, they would say, 'Hello' and they would wave their hands and that was my first impression. When I first came here we joined the Chinese Association of Woking but I made friends with some other Chinese.
Esther Chan

We come from one of the poorest areas in the centre of Sicily, there's hardly anything there. I'm talking about my parents now because I was too small to know. The only work they had was mining, salt for mining but that shut in the early- to mid-'60s and after that, there was only farming there. That's why we had to emigrate. My older brother was here; we decided to reunite all the family and come here.

The first impression when I came out of the plane, it was this dreary atmosphere, we're not used to this in Sicily, and I thought, 'Oh my God, what's going on here?' But once I saw all the trees – we don't have that in Sicily, green is very rare everything is dry – that was the first effect: alright, that's not too bad after all going to Woking.

Mainly the Italians when they first got here they were working in farms, because obviously we came from farming place in Sicily or hospitals as cleaners and anything else.

My parents were waiting for me to get married so they could go back home. I think they stayed eight years and they just went the day after I got married – they couldn't wait. They didn't like it basically.

At nineteen I had my own business and you have to go around and always working. Where I come from, it doesn't work like that – okay, all the people that work, so if something happens, if there's a wedding, they just don't go to work. They phone the boss and say, 'I'm not coming today.' It's a completely different style of life that's there.
Pino Aina

Yes, I hated it to begin with, I don't mind telling you, because I knew nothing. It was hard, it was really hard. I was miserable and wanted to go back – I kept blaming my mum.

As for the country I liked it, it was much better than my town. It was more advanced. Yeah, like washing machines and all these things which we didn't have over there. Like water every day or main gas – it is gas bottles over there – and all these things, so life was a lot easier here. I was here and I thought there was no point in being ignorant. So the best way is to learn and mix with people, which did me good really.
Calogera Morreale

A member of the Italian Community pricking out plants at Pyrford, 1966.
Emilia Aina

When I returned home from my military service I brought some money home which I had saved. I said to my brother, 'We cannot survive with just a donkey,' so we bought a mule. My brother continued to work the land and I found some work in the forest using the mule to load the wood that the workers cut and I transported it to the road where it was made ready for the lorries to take away. Then the boss sold the wood and paid me on an ad hoc basis when I asked him for some money. He wrote down what he owed and how much I was to be paid.

He told us that in England they were looking for workers as there were few people left after the War and there was a lot of work to do.

I made the journey on the train. That took me four days. The railway was all broken from the War and they had not repaired it. The lines that they had mended were the ones for France and Germany but the others were not. I got a direct train for France and then to Calais.

He gave me a banana, I did not know about bananas, we did not have them in Italy. I started eating it with a knife.

I was the only one from my village but the train was full with everyone standing. Everybody was going towards England. People who had been prisoners of war came to fetch their wives and people who had permission like myself who were making their way to England for the first time. When the train stopped in a station and we wanted some water we did not dare leave our place in case we lost it. People were sleeping on the floor, suitcases everywhere. If you wanted to go to the toilet it was almost impossible for fear of stepping on this one or that one. When I arrived at Victoria in London my wife's uncle was waiting for me. He suggested we had a cup of tea and I did not know about tea in those days. At that time he gave me a banana, I did not know about bananas, we did not have them in Italy. I started eating it with a knife and my wife's uncle laughed because he could not believe that in Italy we did not know what a banana was. I then ate it with my hands, but I did not like the taste very much either.
Antonio Falsetta

'Let me go in England. If I have a fortune I will marry you, but if no fortune I back again to Italy.' So, I have a little fortune. In England, work in hospital, work at James Walker.

When I arrived because it was January, the rain, little bit, look like rice, never see before. So I look, it was freezing. Nearly, nearly I back. I catch ship. I take a ship back but I say, 'Well, let me see what is next.' But when I left the port England started nice. It starting to see the house, the road, nice road. But my problem, just I confused and stop. Confused and stop because, I used to drive on the right-hand side and all the time, in the junction I make a mistake but the English understand because I have the Italian number plate. They understand, 'He's come from Italy.' 'Be careful!' No, just I confused and stop. Confused and stop because, in the meantime, I talk to myself, you know? 'Open your eyes, look what you're doing before you move the car. Look at the traffic.' I talk to myself.
Luigi D'Antonio

I come to this country on very famous day, Christmas Day 1968. I suppose they want me to know a better country, to work for and have a better life. That's what they really want, you know?

There was the school nearly three miles away from us, at that time. And then we have the sheep, well, my father had the sheep. I was sheep man. It was great fun not being involved with school education and things like that. When you are young you never think about the education.

Altogether we had four brothers and three sisters and we living in a village called Gurhamatayn. My parents are farmers, they kept the land so they worked there. They all live in Pakistan. My brothers and sisters, they all married. They have their own families and they have tractors. And one of them has a van to drive people around, one worked with my father and middle one he have the farm machine. He's helping but has separate his own business like. He actually grow the chickens as well. He has quite a lot of chickens.

There was the school nearly three miles away from us, at that time. And then we have the sheep, well, my father had the sheep. I was sheep man. It was great fun not being involved with school education and things like that. When you are young you never think about the education.
Mohammed Afsar

A requirement of the job was that the person should be fluent in Urdu and Punjabi, multi-language plus English and with the computer skills. So, I gained that background plus I want to help the community became of the main objective, to help the community who suffer from this barrier of the language. I came to fill that gap to help the community here.

When I joined police, I was a little concerned – 'How they will accept me?' But I fit in very nicely and everybody very helpful. And now the community, they accept me.

I find the police is very helpful because, when I joined police, I was a little concerned – 'How they will accept me?' But I fit in very nicely and everybody very helpful. And now the community, they accept me and have been very helpful as well because they saw this person belongs to them. Yes, so they are open-minded and they come around and talk to me. They can talk anything they want and they seem very friendly and open.
Sultan Khan

I was born in India because my grand-father came from Nepal to join the British East Indian Company's army in the 1900s, and then his children got married and also joined the army, so I was born in 1946 abroad in the British Raj, just before India became independent. My mother was a midwife in the 10th Gurkha Rifles because all the male people in the family, the majority of them, joined the regiments, the British Indian army regiment. So I grew up actually in British Army camp in British Far Eastern Colonies with Gurkhas. Gurkhas serve in British Army, so it was mainly Nepal within British Army camps. It was much easier in the sense that we had running water, we had bed, we had light, whereas in Nepal and the inward villages, those especially, we didn't have electricity and running water. Now some of the towns have telephone and electricity, but in the inward villages up in 12–14,000 feet, a bit difficult to get running water and taps running. It's happening now but in those days, talking about the '40s and the '50s, it was very difficult.

I actually saw in the fog part of the shadow of Houses of Parliament and that was indescribable because I was seeing something I only saw in photographs and Waterloo I thought it was a battleground.

I didn't want to join the army if I could do something totally different than fighting. Then I looked for careers in the army library in Singapore, British Army library, and the nearest I could get into was nursing training, and that fitted me all right.

The idea was to come and train in England, get my qualification and probably go round the world in English speaking countries like Canada, Australia, New Zealand and then go back to Nepal. So the British doctors in the Camp helped me to find a hospital. I had many, many choices but somehow Chertsey became the choice.

I was seeing things that I had only read in history books.

So I flew to Brize Norton. I looked out; it was bitterly cold, it was foggy, the plane only landed at the third attempt otherwise we had to go to Scotland, Prestwick. I was seeing things that I only read in history books. One of the things I wanted to do was to see the Houses of Parliament and the Tower of London. That was lucky and on the way from Paddington to Waterloo I actually saw in the fog part of the shadow of Houses of Parliament and that was indescribable because I was seeing something I only saw in photographs and Waterloo I thought it was a battleground. So I came to Chertsey and registered myself with the police in Addlestone and then the introduction to Woking was partly through the training we had to do.

My mother told me that I would settle all right in the sense that I like potatoes, so she said I wouldn't miss rice much because I like potatoes. Winter time, I felt quite cold, the first two years, it took me some time to get used to the weather in the sense that it was quite cold. I used to put a jumper underneath the white top the male nurse had to wear because the first two years I really felt cold because I wasn't brought up in Nepal, I was brought up in the tropics so, yes, the first two winters were very trying. But I was a very outgoing, happy go lucky chap, so summertime I used to get on the bike and go round

Windsor Castle and things like that. I used to cycle all the way.

Then I met my wife. Maya is from Holland but I met her in England and then Woking more or less became a home for us, so we got married and she came here and joined me. And we have been living in Knaphill since 1975.
Raj Chhetri

Ghurkhas with snake *Jenny Marley*

When the girls come here, believe it or not, or the boys come here – they say, 'Oh my God, we're cooped up, there's nowhere to go, four walls, what do you do here?'

I just didn't like Woking. I said, 'I'm not staying here.' He says, 'Let's go and have a look, don't just put your mind to one thing, let's go and have a look.' When we get off the train there was no shopping here, because you have a wider choice in London, it's a big city and there was nothing here. Then we got another house, it was a two bedroom house and about that time, I already had a daughter and she was sent to Pakistan because I was working and there was no one here to look after her. So she had to come back to Woking because she went away when she was nine months, and when she came back, she was nearly quarter to three years old. It's very difficult to think about how one can carry on with life working and looking after a child, and I had to give up work to look after her and then I started doing little work.

Back home, they don't have dining tables to sit on because in the Muslim world, you segregate the men and the women. So the men and the boys are given food before the ladies and the girls. Here in the dining room, they would all sit together – that was confusing for those children. There's so many things. The ladies – because I said they were farmers – when they first came, they didn't know how to light the cooker, because they were not used to having cookers at home, they always burnt firewood to cook. They had to go to wells to take water, here everybody's got a tap. When the girls come here, believe it or not, or the boys come here – they say, 'Oh my God, we're cooped up, there's nowhere to go, four walls, what do you do here?' It's a different way of life completely.
Rafeea Mahoon

Initially I joined the Army, I was given a Commission and then we worked on a lot of road making in the Azad/Kashmir area and then I was selected – in fact, I was the first Pakistani officer to come to England on a course. I mean as the first Pakistani as Engineer Officer, to make it quite clear, for a two year course to Loughborough and we studied works management and workshop training and that's how I came to meet Dolores.

Well, it's so funny because I got married and before '50 we were not allowed to marry foreigners. So I was on a punishment posting to another rather remote part of Pakistan called Shinkiari and we were posted there for two years almost. There again, it was a very idyllic spot, it was fairly high in the mountains, very pleasant area and, in fact, no hardship at all to us.
Brigadier Muslim Salamat

But as far as adjusting culture-wise was concerned or the way of people and their behaviour and all that is concerned, it was very different. Because I could speak the language, so I didn't find it very difficult. Their attitudes, their way of life, the religious differences, they do upset you a lot, they do make you very upset. Culturally it was very very hard.

As far as adjusting culture-wise was concerned, it was very different. Their attitudes, their way of life, the religious differences, they do make you very upset. Culturally it was very very hard.

In earlier days, of course every single thing was different, down to just a small detail like if you were cooking in the kitchen, and also cleaning in the house was very different as well. You use obviously brushes and other kind of things to clean in Pakistan but here, you had to use a hoover. Although we had hoover in Pakistan as well but still it's different here. The one interesting thing is that there are no drains in the toilets and in the kitchen and we are so used to cleaning your kitchen and toilet floor with water. I must say that I flooded the bathroom floor once, because I thought there's got to be a drain here and also did exactly the same with the kitchen floor and my husband told me that, no, you have to mop everything up and suck the water with the help of this cloth and that was quite interesting and annoying, but that is what I found very different. How can you clean a kitchen floor and a toilet floor without having a drain there and really using lots of water instead of just using a mop? But now it makes sense.

I must say that I flooded the bathroom floor once, because I thought there's got to be a drain here and also did exactly the same with the kitchen floor.

I think I used to go to the bank and pay there in the bank, sometimes in the post office because I had my accounts I think soon as I came here. After a few months, I opened my own account along with my husband, so it wasn't that difficult, just go

down to the bank and pay the bill. I actually found it quite interesting and quite nice. I was only twenty-one at that time but I found it quite interesting and quite exciting that I could do these things myself, while back home, I had never ever done these kind of things. I don't have to go and pay the bills and even go and fetch money from my bank account. So all these things I was doing myself, but I found it was a good opportunity for me to do things for myself and quite easily. They're quite nice systems here – the whole set up is quite easy. It's accessible for everybody, every common person, now I know that you don't even have to be really highly educated to do this kind of stuff really; it's ever so easy for everybody, they can do it.
Ghazala Waheed

I mean, in summer here I still have problems because I don't like the heat. Yes, the only thing is the houses are very close and, I think, that's what was strange. They're close, they're shut all the way round. In Pakistan it's open houses so, in other words, you're cooking in the garden whereas here you go to relax in the garden.

We had an arranged marriage. Yes, our marriage was arranged. My husband was in Pakistan, I was in England. The first time we saw each other was when I went to Pakistan in '90. That was the first time I went back and we got married. I was quite happy for that. My husband's life was totally different, opposite to the life I had led in the sense that my husband comes from a village and I was brought up in a city and then I was in England. I had spent my life in England as an independent woman by the time I married him and his life was very different because he was living in a village.

When I got married and I found myself in my husband's house it was very different but when you step into a life that's very different it can be very exciting because it's new for me because suddenly I was experimenting with new things. Suddenly there wasn't water in the house. We had to go to a well to get it and that was very different and I found it very strange as well as very exciting because all the village ladies used to get together and go to the well to get water, which wasn't an experience that I'd been used to living in England. By the time I'd got married, I'd spent fifteen or twenty-odd years here. It was very different, we were all living in one house, sharing facilities with his married brother with children and his sisters.

I didn't have any problems where his family was concerned. They were really good. They looked after me but, like I said, I was a very independent woman here. I was working, I had my own car. I was driving, I was making decisions for myself and then life in Pakistan was very different because people have their own way of thinking. They have their certain restrictions.

Pakistani life in the open air: Nighat Jobeen's house *Nighat Jobeen*

The ladies lead a very social life, you'll be surprised to know. On a Friday everybody goes to the Mosque to pray. Weekends the children go to Urdu school so that's where all the children meet. In the evenings they have Islamic Studies, that's where they meet. We have a very open house policy. You don't make an appointment to go round somebody's house. You just go and people expect that and people expect to come and visit you. I used to find that very strange and, I think, I still do now. You know, where parents ask their children whether they go round. The children say and vice versa, 'Can we come round this weekend or tomorrow?' 'Can we have dinner?' It's not like that with Asian communities. It's an open door policy. You go, you visit, if you arrive there at lunch time you have lunch. If you arrive at tea time you have tea. It's a very social and very close-knit community.

When we first came here people used to say, 'Ugh, the smell of curry here. We don't like it and you smell and the house smells.' And now they know more about our dishes than we do. So, that's where food is concerned, you know? Now English people will say, 'Can we have samosas and can we have this or that?' And they know more about food and about culture I think. Where racism is concerned it just depends on what community and what part of the country you're living in. In Woking, where communities are concerned, you know, this part of Woking, Maybury, maybe it's not as bad other parts. Yes, there is racism but, then again, I think it's lack of knowledge, lack of understanding. And media and television really take it out of proportion.
Nighat Jobeen

The houses are very close and, that's what was strange. They're shut all the way round. In Pakistan it's open houses.

Nighat Jobeen's open plan house
Nighat Jobeen

Yes, there is racism but I think it's lack of knowledge, lack of understanding. And media and television really take it out of proportion.

Exciting in the sense that schools were well-equipped and huge buildings, which we were not used to and teachers were different in methods of teaching as well and most of all the discipline was low, so that was exciting as far as I was concerned! You didn't have the punishments for not learning what we were accustomed to, that if you didn't do your homework you were punished.

It is a difficult balance but it is to accept, I think, to accept the good practices of this country and its people and reject the bad practices of this country and its people. While at the same time accept the good practices of being a Muslim and the bad practices of being a Pakistani or Asian. There are some good and bad in every culture and it is to accept the good is a greater challenge. The commercial pressures in the modern world are so great and there are huge problems within our own community with regards to lots of issues, it's to address them, and people like myself will try and take on these challenges but it's not us alone that make the difference. And so I look at it with a lot of optimism that we can achieve this.

I find that the opportunities for young children, especially young Muslim children, are great. They have to stop looking at themselves in an inward manner and look at it in an outward manner, whilst not forgetting who they are, what their fathers were, what they are all about.

One of the beauties of this country has been its ability to accept other cultures and other religions and I admire that within the British people, but I see in the modern trend a certain extreme element that's creeping in. But the ability and the beauty of the British people is their ability to accept others and I think that is one of their greatest strengths and I must admit that's what makes them richer for it and their progress. This is the secret of their progress and I admire that immensely.
Shamas Tabrez

One of the beauties of this country has been its ability to accept other cultures and other religions and I admire that within the British people.

I would say there's some people that think backwards in a way, to the way that Muslim girls should be in Woking. Because some of the guys in Woking think that girls should stay at home, they shouldn't be out of the house, they should be covered, cooking, cleaning. Then again, it's like the guys' opinion, it's okay for them to go out and drink and socialise but it's not alright for girls.
Rehana Kauser

We should like get involved in each other more, as we are one community. There should be more things for children, activities for Muslim children. There can be white people as well. More children's activities like play schemes in Maybury Centre. I don't know if there's already one there like for Muslims, coloured people. And they should talk to each other about any problems and we can deal with them.
Student

We should like get involved in each other more, as we are one community.

We used to go from
Goldsworth School over the
stepbridge and see the horses
dragging the barges along.

I remember the canal freezing and my father making me skates to skate on it. I remember swimming in the canal.

2. Out of Doors

I never spoke to the boatmen. I think they must have lived on these barges because the front end of the barge used to have a little chimney stuck out the top of the cab and there was smoke coming out of there sometimes in the winter.

So we went up to play on the barges and what did I do? I fell in the canal! In the new suit – the first time I'd worn it and the only suit I'd ever had. I couldn't swim.

I absolutely love fishing so I just spent all day fishing and things like that really. We would play games like any other kids, cowboys and indians, and used to make bows and arrows from the hedgerows. We'd often dam streams. In fact, there are some streams in nearby West End that we would fish in. If we'd get fed up with the fishing, damming streams was a good alternative, always.
Pete Garland

My childhood seemed to be full of summer days playing and having a great time and especially being in the woods. When my cousin, who also lived in Knaphill, used to take me out, it was wonderful because she'd show me all the flowers. She showed me the flowers and the birds; we'd sit together in the woods at the bottom of Lower Guildford Road (which is now an industrial estate). I remember in there was a lake and we'd sit there and watch the kingfishers for hours.

My Auntie lived in Victoria Road and her house backed onto the woods. I remember staying there and the owls used to come and sit on the windowsill. We'd always sleep with the curtains open so that if the owls came we could see them.
Jennifer Wharam

It was a cottage with a long garden and at the end of the garden there was a hedge through which there was a wonderful field that seemed to belong to me, 'my buttercup field.' I remember the ecstasy I had when finding a double buttercup in 'my' buttercup field.
Barbara Elton

We used to spend a lot of time over Wisley Common. We'd never come home empty handed, we'd always bring a lump of wood home and cut it up for the fire. We were always doing something to help the house carry on. In the summer you were out in the garden weeding or watering, or whatever and then in the evenings, well, you'd just sit and read you see. We had a radio that worked some times and not others, but I don't think we're any worse off for it, quite frankly.
Geoffrey Simpson

My childhood seemed to be full of summer days playing and having a great time and especially being in the woods.

We used to do a lot of skipping and hopscotch. We played on the dirt, on the playground or in the garden on the path. We played that and marbles, conkers and 'tracks'. We used to make arrows in the dirt with sticks and with a bit through the middle to show which way you went. And when you got to the end you used to make a round and put 'H' in it for 'home.' You used to go and hide, and they had to come and find you, following the arrows. We'd play this on the green or anywhere and just hide in hedges around.
Elsie Goff

Children playing in sandpits on Horsell Common, c. 1930s.
Mollie Elborn

Horse riders on Horsell Common, c. 1940s
Bernadette Rivett

We'd play hopscotch and skipping, and two balls and five stones. Also swapping beads. Nice games though.

Up Albert Drive on the left hand side was a wood. I called it 'The Bluebell Wood' and I took my sisters there. We found a bit of tree and would sit under it. It was our camp. I remember the smell of all those ferns.

If we jumped our fence we were in the canal. We used to swing across but only when it got down. If you fell in you'd just be smelly and your Mum would tell you off but you couldn't drown. It was sludge.
Sandra Thurling

We were running round the woods and making camps and exploring and of course there was the Muslim burial ground (on Horsell Common) which was about I suppose a couple of hundred yards from our home in the woods and so that acted really as the north west frontier. We were running round it and we were firing through the slots in the brickwork or pretending to, so it was like a film set for us.
David Evans

I remember the gypsies being on Horsell Common. I don't remember seeing their encampments but they came and they camped. The gypsy children, who were always very beautiful, would come to the door and ask for a jug of milk.
Bernadette Rivett

As boys we spent our lives on Horsell Common. There was no question of television or radio or anything else, you just made your own pleasure, which we all did in those days. We went on the common in summer or whenever it was, collecting wood, playing games, everything.
Sir Alec Bedser

If you stood with your back to The Cricketers (public house), you could see right across to the boundary trees over at the far side by Carthouse Lane. There was just heather because it got burnt off about every other year. But over on it there'd been any amount of excavations, certainly not for building material, because it wasn't that sort of ground, but because of the comparative freshness then I should think they were just exercises by the military for the First War and never filled in. They were great for us kids, you could do all sorts of things in this and we used to run all over this area. We would make a camp in them and have battles with catapults with each other. There were some good climbing trees there. We would be exploring all the time because everyone had bicycles.
Derek Haycroft

A plane came down near Street's Heath – what is the recreation ground at West End now. It crashed down there. The two that were in it left the plane to crash and bailed out with parachutes. They were picked up on Horsell Common.
Elsie Goff

Where the Woking High School is now, you could stand and look out and see nothing but heath for miles. It was flat, it was gorse and bracken. During the Blitz you could stand at the end of Morton Road and look out over Horsell Common and see the red of the fires burning in London. On the night of the Great Fire, the 29th December 1940, when you get that picture of St. Paul's, I went to a dance. There was this dreadful bombing going on, and my father came to fetch me and we walked back to Horsell and the sky was not red, it was white. I always remember that, white sky from the fierceness of the fires and we were twenty-five miles from London.
Bernadette Rivett

Old Forge at Cheapside, Horsell Common, 1940s
Bernadette Rivett

When it was time to clean the large carpet my grandfather took it up the road in his Martynside motor bike and sidecar and dragged it through the heather on the common, as a way of cleaning the carpet.
Terry Fuller

We really used to go to Boundary Common, when we got a little bit older. (If you come into Woking from the Six Crossroads as you hit Woking there's a large roundabout there. That, on the right hand side, you can still see part of a green, if you like.) That was quite a large area and had a football pitch on it. That's where we used to play football. But that was the main focal point of the Maybury boys, what we called the 'Walton Road area boys.'
Richard Wooller

I remember the canal freezing and my father making me skates to skate on it. I remember swimming in the canal.
Barbara Chasemore

I remember the canal freezing and my father making me skates to skate on it. I remember swimming in the canal.

We played in the streets, Walton Road and that area. We used to go over to Spanton's, where the canal is. There used to be a big wood factory there. I went over there playing one Saturday and I was three and I had wellingtons on because the grass was wet and we went round the back of Spanton's, right along by the canal bank and I fell in. I can remember going under the water and seeing all the reeds. There was a boy called Lenny Parker lived next door to my grandmother. He and his brother were there with us. He pulled me up by my hair, took me home and my grandma gave me a walloping that I'll never forget. I never went near the canal again. Not that part anyway.
Pamela Peachey

Ice-skating on Basingstoke Canal, 1962
Ann Squibb

Spanton's timber yard, 1972 *Philip J. Moll*

Just by the Monument Bridge, the town side, the coal barges used to unload coal, I suppose it was for the gasworks that used to be down there. We used to swim in the canal there because where they'd unloaded the coal off the barges. A certain amount used to fall in the water and it formed a nice sort of firm spot – the bottom of your feet weren't sinking in the mud 'cause there was a lot of coal at the bottom.
Bert Hollis

At Belton's Boathouse, you used to be able to go and hire a boat for so much an hour. A rowing boat or a canoe and sometimes a punt, depending what you wanted. No motorised vehicles, all manual with oars.

There used to be a wharf at what is now Harelands and then at Brewster's there was another. By (what is now) the car park up Brewery Road used to be Belton's Boathouse. At Belton's Boathouse, you used to be able to go and hire a boat for so much an hour. A rowing boat or a canoe and sometimes a punt, depending what you wanted. No motorised vehicles, all manual with oars. That was a favourite on Sunday afternoon when you'd earned a few coppers. Just an hour on the canal on a rowing boat was a treat. And then, just a little bit further, between Belton's Boathouse and Brewster's there was another timber yard called Aston Grant's.
Harry Tapley

Punting on the canal *Elsie Miles*

My father worked on the barges, unloading the timber. He started about six o'clock in the morning, came in to breakfast at eight, then worked from eight till twelve and then from twelve till five. They had a plank coming from the barge over the water, over the path into Brewster's. They used to carry the planks of wood on their shoulder. They more or less half ran if you know what I mean. Some wood was on the barges already cut up, but some Brewster's cut themselves which was by machine. The wood was turned into planks, and my grandfather was the head machinist there. He was there over fifty years. They had their own offices in there and my other grandfather worked there as well. So, my mother's father worked there over fifty years, and my other grandfather worked there forty-nine years, and my father worked there about forty-six, so it was quite a long time between them.

Brewster's ran a carnival, which I was in many, many years ago, when the Woking Victoria Hospital wanted funds. It was about the late 1930s. We paraded through the town.
Peggy Goring

Canal barges loaded with timber and workers, c.1930s *Peggy Goring*

Brewsters carnival float, 1934 *Peggy Goring*

We had Brewster's Timber Yard in Arthurs Bridge Road and opposite to that we had what we used to call 'The Logs'. The Logs, well it was logs, it was just that. A man called Chris Spires was the engine driver for Brewster's, an industrial steam engine which towed a trailer. Most mornings, he would be round there to fire up somewhere about five or six o'clock in the morning, so that by seven or eight o'clock he would be ready for the road with Brewster's steam engine and trailer to wherever they were cutting and hauling out timber. He'd come back in the evening, sometimes through Abbey Road and sometimes through Brewery Road, with this trailer load of timber and then we used to go and watch him unload by The Logs (where Bridge Court is today). We used to go round there and play hide-and-seek, all the kids did. That was a favourite play spot.

After they had all gone home, we kids would often go and play on the barges. Sometimes they left the cabins open so that you could go in. They all had a small cabin on these barges. I used to have to go to Sunday School. So, I'm going down the road to meet the people that I used to go to Sunday School with and they're saying, 'Oh we're not going to Sunday School today, we're going up to play on the barges.' So I said, 'Well, that's me as well then!' So we went up to play on the barges and what did I do? I fell in the canal! In the new suit – the first time I'd worn it and the only suit I'd ever had. I couldn't swim, I just managed to get out and they pulled me out by the side of the bank. The barges were moored close to the bank and actually I suppose the depth of the canal wasn't that deep. I suppose I could have walked, but it was deep enough, I could have drowned.
Harry Tapley

So we went up to play on the barges and what did I do? I fell in the canal! In the new suit – the first time I'd worn it and the only suit I'd ever had. I couldn't swim.

If you went up to the top of Arnold Road and you turned right, just before you went over to Monument Bridge, which was always known as Bunker's Bridge, and walked a few yards along the canal, you saw the barges bringing in the coal and the timber which was unloaded onto a little railway track.
If you went up Monument Bridge, on the left and went down to the canal towpath, then go along a couple of hundred yards, there used to be a big crane there. The barges used to come along the canal, some would have timber on and some coal. The coal ones used to pull up at this crane and it took off the coal which used to go to the gasworks that was along there. The coal was unloaded into little trucks on the railway and this was taken to the coke ovens, heated, and the gas went into the holders, because there used to be a big gas holder there. The coke which was left was bagged up and sold to the public. During the War we couldn't get coal. We were allowed a bag a week and used to come once a fortnight and bring two bags.
Betty Curtis

We used to go from Goldsworth School over the bridge and see the horses dragging the barges along.

Old step bridge off Goldsworth Road, 1905 *Philip J. Moll*

We used to go from Goldsworth School over the stepbridge and see the horses dragging the barges along. All the empty barges were stored by Arthurs Bridge. There was a sort of a basin there and they would be there until they got a full one and then the old horse would probably take two barges back.
Doris Francis

The canal was empty for a long, long time. The canal ran through Woodham where we lived. We were told not to play near the canal because it was quite deep but we did. It had kingfishers, swans, ducks, moorhens, newts, tadpoles, lovely rushes and some canal boats. I think lack of maintenance caused it to dry up after the War. The whole canal was totally dry for years and it was growing trees and bushes. It was dry all the way to West Byfleet.
Wendy Davenport

At the Maybury end of the canal was Bunker's Bridge and it was called Bunker's Bridge because when you did cross-country from here you used to run out through the fields, onto the canal, turn left and run up towards Woking. And if you were clever you could hide under the bridge while everyone else ran on for another two miles and, on the way back, you would join the end of the queue and run back into school. So that's why that was called Bunker's Bridge. Bunking off.[1]
Barry Pope

1 Bunker's Bridge was so named in the 1850s when it was a squatter settlement, but the name certainly seems to have acquired this other meaning. (Ed.)

Worker at Spanton's timber yard, 1967
Richard Snell

Oil drum raft c.1970s *Philip J. Moll*

The barges used to come along loaded up with timber and unload at Brewster's. There was another one further along the other side, going out of Woking towards the Six Crossroads, Spanton's. I never spoke to the boatmen. I think they must have lived on these barges because the front end of the barge used to have a little chimney stuck out the top of the cab and there was smoke coming out of there sometimes in the winter. All the wood was along the front part of the barge. They were quite big things. I don't know how many tons of timber they carried but it was quite a considerable load. I never saw them going up St Johns Locks but they turned round just before you got to Arthurs Bridge. There was a wide piece there, and from Brewster's they used to come up, past Brewster's, up to that wide bit to turn the barge round and bring it back. Sometimes they'd go underneath the bridge, and the horse would pull the barge up towards the bridge and the chap in charge of the horse would unhook it quickly and the horse would go over the top because there wasn't room for him to go under the bridge with the barge. There was enough forward momentum so it went through under the bridge on its own and then the horse came over the top, and met it the other side and coupled up again. The men wore ordinary working men's clothes.
Bert Hollis

I never spoke to the boatmen. I think they must have lived on these barges because the front end of the barge used to have a little chimney stuck out the top of the cab and there was smoke coming out of there sometimes.

There was a raft that the workmen had built. It was just a wooden platform with sort of five gallon oil drums fixed underneath and there was a chain at each end. They used to pull themselves across the canal on it.

One of my favourite occupations was fishing in the canal. I had a friend down the bottom of Vale Farm Road; near the back of that place was Mr May. He had a forge. I remember going in there and the horrible smell of burning hoof, he'd be shoeing horses. I also remember I wanted a fishing rod and they were half a crown, 2/6d, but I could never. We used to go along the canal bank towards St Johns and where they've built Goldsworth Park now, that used to be Slocock's Nursery, and just along there was a raft that the workmen had built. It was just a wooden platform with sort of five gallon oil drums fixed underneath and there was a chain at each end. They used to pull themselves across the canal on it because Slocock's Nurseries was either side of the canal. So we used to wait until the workmen came over, they'd put their barrows on this raft and shovels and everything, their tools, pull it across the canal and they used to go and work over on the Horsell side of the nursery there during the day. And when we saw them go over there, we used to nip on the raft, pull it across and they grew lovely tall canes, about eight or nine foot tall, and we used to pinch a couple of these canes, back across the canal, we used to tie our line on the end and use them as fishing rods.
Bert Hollis

It's a nice community, and at Christmas we all get together in the nursery, and we're still all good friends and I'm still 'Mr Martin'.

Everybody during the War wanted to buy fruit trees and there was a huge overstock at the end of it because people suddenly stopped buying them.

There was a time when Woking grew probably nearly a half of the trees and shrubs raised in the whole of the United Kingdom.

3. Pots and Plants

The men tended to stay in the business for all of their lives. I think that would have been true in any walk of life. People didn't move from one job to another.

Working Knaphill Nursery with both horse-drawn plough and JCB c.1960
Surrey History Centre

Woking was agricultural. There were Slocock's, Knaphill and Jackman's Nurseries. These were famous nurseries and they imported workers from Italy, Sicily and Spain. This is the reason for the large Italian community around here now.
Wendy Davenport

The nursery was known as Goldsworth Nursery and the history goes back to 1760, when the nursery was started, originally I think by a chap called Turner who went through rather difficult times in the early nineteenth century. My grandfather, Walter Charles, decided he wanted to be a nurseryman and came to Knaphill Nursery to learn the trade of horticulture under, I think it was then Gomer Waterer. After training there he went abroad and trained a bit more on the continent and then came back in to the nursery and took it over in 1887. From then on it was one long success story.

Goldsworth House c.1950 *Martin Slocock*

My father was a nurseryman. He read Botany in Oxford (as did I) and came back to join his brother in the business. But my grandfather died in 1926 so my father was not here at the nursery for very long while his father was alive.

There was a time when Woking grew probably nearly a half of the trees and shrubs raised in the whole of the United Kingdom. It was by far Woking's largest industry and largest source of employment.

There was a time shortly after my grandfather died when Woking grew probably nearly a half of the trees and shrubs raised in the whole of the United Kingdom. It was by far Woking's largest industry and largest source of employment. That was the source of its prosperity before the railway came in and the proximity of London meant that there are other places to go to work. It was a really labour–intensive occupation anyway, prior to mechanisation and weed-killing. When I joined the nursery we employed a hundred and twenty people, before that there were two hundred or three hundred. These were permanent, not seasonal workers. We bought and built quite a lot of houses so a lot of our staff were actually living on the land.

The centre, the heartland, of the nursery was Goldsworth House, which is the house in which my grandfather and grandmother lived. My grandmother died in 1943. She very much kept the family together when her young sons joined the business in the '20s and '30s. She was still very much in charge – Sophia. The Goldsworth area was strictly speaking south of the canal. We then extended right up to the Littlewick Road and over towards Chobham. My father and brother had purchased quite a large area of land from the Waterers, in Knaphill Nursery, in 1936. Some of that was used for the production of trees, fruit and Christmas trees and other parts of it were used as a farm where we raised cattle and we all know the best source of nitrogen comes from cattle! That was how we used the land, to fatten cattle, cattle to get all the farmyard manure we wanted.

We had a dairy herd at Harelands. (I think it's Harelands Close just near on the north side of the canal, and that was Harelands Farm.) It was run by an irascible farmer for us, Mr Warren. He brought up the milk twice a day. We always knew it had been milked by Mr Warren because it always had cigarette ash in it because it had been done in the proper way! Each

member of the family had his own churn which was delivered to the office in the afternoon. Nobody ever took anybody else's churn. It was milk you could stand a spoon up in. I mean, no doubt all the doctors would say we should have died of cholesterol poisoning a long time ago, but it was wonderful milk, nobody skimmed anything off, it was glorious!

When I came back to the nursery I was tossed in at the deep end. I was given a large part of the nursery to look after, the piece over towards Chobham which we still own. We had about a hundred and twenty staff, and there were some very experienced foremen. Again, generations of foremen had worked for us. We were very, very fortunate in the quality of the staff and the employees we had. So there were some pretty old heads that showed me what to do but I was responsible for the day-to-day management of this particular area. We started at seven o'clock in the morning, broke for breakfast at nine. We started again at half-past nine, and

Preparation of a cedar tree for the Air Ministry, Knaphill Nursery, 1938
Martin Slocock

A large tree being loaded onto a trailer, 1960s *Martin Slocock* worked till twelve. Then the men worked from one till five, and I went on deep into the night, as I remember, and then started again the next morning, working Saturday mornings as well.

The busiest time of the year was October, November and December because everyone at that stage bought trees and shrubs in the autumn. They didn't buy them in containers from garden centres. Then there was a bit of a lull before another burst in February, March. After March all the lifting and dispatch of plants stopped. And then we went on with the other work of budding and grafting and pruning and weeding and things like that.

The Chobham end was mainly growing fruit, and also had a large agricultural holding. That's where we fattened all our two hundred beef. They all had to come

up to Woking on railway trucks. We unloaded them just off Poole Road, and we drove them, literally up the Goldsworth Road. We're talking of the late '50s and early '60s. I mean, imagine driving cattle up the Goldsworth Road now!

We made a lot of hay to supply our cattle and also our carthorses. We also used to grow rye, the reason being that rye produces a very long straw. We wanted the longest straw we could get to use for packing trees. The straw was brought in, not in bales, but in the old-fashioned stooks, so sheaves of rye straw used to come in and we used that rye straw to wrap round the trees to protect the stems in transit. I remember growing rye into the mid-'60s.

Looking back to the time before I arrived, I'm told that some of our produce

used to go onto the canal. When I arrived we had four very hefty lorries and that's how it was mainly sent out. But we also had a lot of carthorses. We had carthorses until the early '90s. In addition to lorries, it was sent by rail. A lot of stock we would deliver to the station.

Alf Carey used to leave the nursery about the end of May, early June and used to go and cut bracken with a long-handled scythe on the common land around Chobham. We used to collect it, bring it in and that was the packing material we used to keep the roots moist. My grandfather even started making bricks at the old Chobham Brickworks and built his houses out of bricks he made at Chobham. Certainly it was a nicely joined-up industry.

They all had to come up to Woking on railway trucks. We unloaded them just off Poole Road, and we drove them, literally up the Goldsworth Road. I mean, imagine driving cattle up the Goldsworth Road now!

There were huge osier beds. I mentioned the rye straw and I mentioned the bracken, but we used to grow our own osiers, to tie up the trees – trees were never tied up with string. It's much quicker to tie up trees, or a bundle of any kind, if you know how, with an osier. One loop at the thick end, you whip through the thin end, one turn, two turns and it's done. I don't remember ever seeing a ball of string before I believe the late 1970s.

In those days trees were usually grown to the length of about fourteen feet overall. They were all sent bare root, so you could get huge quantities of trees on a

lorry. We were the largest of the four principal nurseries, wholesale nurseries round Woking. There was Hilling's in Chobham, Fromow's over towards Windlesham, and also Roseland in Chobham. Very little of our trade was retail customers.

In 1970 my father died, so I was only thirty-five when I was left holding the baby. We were then subjected to a compulsory purchase order for the whole of Goldsworth and quite a lot of the land extending behind St Johns towards Knaphill. Other members of my family still had interests in the nursery land so it was a family decision we had to make. We spent quite a lot of time between 1970 and 1974 talking to different large developers. We then established a relationship with Trafalgar House and it was on that basis that we developed the land and Goldsworth Park came into existence. For many, many years I never drove through Goldsworth Park. I do now, but it took me years to get used to seeing areas of land and oak trees under which I had stood and shot pigeon, surrounded by houses. There were many parts of the nursery which were more special than others. All of them had wonderful names: Lock Field, which is now perpetuated in Lockfield Drive, but it was known as Lock Field; Renshaw's because Renshaw worked there; the Square; Oldforce meadow; Burgefield. But all the names given to the fields were because there was some feature in them which lent attribution, or it was named after people who always worked there.

Goldsworth Park was developed over a number of years and the withdrawal was timetabled in such a way that we released land to Trafalgar House so that we would stay in Goldsworth House, which had its greenhouses and all our dispatch yards, until the last minute. It became increasingly difficult to run a nursery which became so fragmented that the lines of communication within it became difficult. So in 1976 I took the view that we really had to organise ourselves in a different way. We had retained all the land north of Carthouse Lane; that was really as I called it the Chobham end, although strictly speaking it's in Horsell – the Chobham end went right over to Bisley.

Knaphill Nursery had been in the Waterer family for nine generations since 1795. To cut a long story short, I bought Knaphill Nursery in 1976. We were then able to transfer the office and the dispatch and the HQ of the nursery from Goldsworth House and the immediate area to Knaphill Nursery. We reorganised ourselves, because Knaphill was essentially a retail business, and therefore we made the switch from a largely wholesale business to a retail business. My father had largely been responsible for Slocock's specialising in rhododendrons. He bred a lot of rhododendrons, many of which carry my family's name, and after the War we continued this and put up a lot of exhibits at Chelsea which won a lot of prizes for rhododendrons, while Knaphill had become famous for azaleas. So the natural marriage, if ever there was one, was of rhododendrons and azaleas: we became a centre for the production of rhododendrons and azaleas.

In the late 1970s and the 1980s all sorts of other materials became available. Transport became more efficient, so that you weren't sending trees by rail but by lorry. So all the practices of cutting fern, cutting osiers and cutting rye for protecting stems, all this is a happy memory.

We continued our wholesale production for some time, but in the latter stages of the 1980s and 1990s we really started concentrating more on the retail sale than on wholesale. Increasingly plants began to be put in pots and we started container

production, so the whole pattern of the massive dispatch session, the lifting of plants and dispatch and assembly of orders in the autumn has really now gone.

He bred a lot of rhododendrons, many of which carry my family's name. After the War we continued and put up exhibits at Chelsea which won a lot of prizes.

It was clear that my sons were not going to go into the business so I sold the garden centre which I had developed at Knaphill and which was all of our own making, but retained all the other land. We still grow rhododendrons and azaleas, really that's our concentration. There will come a time when I will retire. We will keep all our rhododendrons, keep all our collections, but in terms of production that will be the end of the Slocock era in horticulture. I've done fifty years and one faces reality. But it's been good fun.

The trees on the land that I own here in Knaphill are wonderful. They were planted mainly in the 1820s to 1840s and many of them are the largest trees of their kind in the country. For example, the weeping beech (which now occupies about half an acre of land and features in all sorts of books on specimen trees) and the largest cut-leaf beech. We also have the original of a number of conifers, including the original pine – Waterer, pinus silvestris waterii – which was bred here. On the rhododendron front there is a rhododendron catawbiense, which was grown from seed collected by John Fraser on the Catawbe River and reputedly planted here in 1815. So you can imagine the horticultural pedigree of some of the plants here. James Burchett was my father's first rhododendron foreman and that's a lovely late-flowering rhododendron. And there's Faggetter's Favourite (Faggetter was the foreman before him). I like to think that their names as well as their memories will live on.

My father and I were active, as it were, in horticulture. We both worked hard for our respective trade bodies and over the last thirty-two years I have been on the Council for the Royal Horticultural Society. I retired in 2002 after ten years as Treasurer.

It's a nice community, and at Christmas we all get together in the nursery, and we're still all good friends and I'm still 'Mr Martin'.

When we withdrew from Goldsworth there was inevitably some loss of jobs but not many. For many years we have been able to house many of our staff in Woking. I bought some more houses in Knaphill, on the ground near Chobham to house them, as we do to this day. And we house their widows as well. I'm sorry to say that some of the splendid chaps who worked for me and my father have inevitably passed on, but their widows are very often hale and hearty and they still live in our houses. It's a nice community, and at Christmas we all get together in the nursery, and we're still all good friends and I'm still 'Mr Martin'.
Martin Slocock

CLOCKWISE FROM TOP LEFT:

Three female hoers at Jackmans Nursery, 1930s *Mr & Mrs Coombs*

Haymakers at Jackmans Nursery, 1930s *Mr & Mrs Coombs*

Bound trees at Jackmans Nursery, 1930s *Mr & Mrs Coombs*

Frank Burchett, fruit foreman at Jackmans Nursery, 1930s *Mr & Mrs Coombs*

I knew I wanted to work in horticulture because I had worked on Saturdays and holidays at a little nursery.
I went to Jackman's Nursery and thought that I might go to college later. But I just stayed at Jackman's and learnt through the practical side of it. In those days I used to cycle to work 'cause on a wage of about £5.10s.0d a week you couldn't really afford much else. Everybody cycled, one or two people had real old motor bikes but the only people that had cars were Mr Jackman himself and the Company Secretary.

In those days it was all grown in the ground and they had what was known as the stock ground, which was a sort of fully grown sample of one of everything that Jackman's grew. Customers made appointments with Mr Arthur Tomes and he took them round the stock ground. They'd say, 'I've got a huge sunny garden and I want to fill it with shrubs, what are the best sort of things?' and he'd go through a list with them and he could take them round the stock ground and show them. They ordered the plants throughout the year but they couldn't have them until what was known as the 'lifting season' which was usually in November but it was weather dependent (when everything went dormant). Lifting went on usually until about the end of March. They had a despatch system from the office down where the greenhouses were. (Jackman's had a few acres that backed onto Evelyn Close – near Wych Hill – which was where they had the remainders of the glasshouses and the potting sheds and they grew all the alpines and climbing plants.) Of course every plant was under its Latin name.

In those days I cycled to work 'cause on a wage of £5.10s.od a week you couldn't afford much else. Everybody cycled, one or two people had real old motor bikes but the only people that had cars were Mr Jackman himself and the Company Secretary.

The bamboos and pampas grass were huge great bushy plants. When we used to get the orders for the pampas grass we had to dig them up. It used to take two of you because of the tough roots. We used to break them in half, one half for the customer and the other half we'd plant back in the ground again for next year's stock. A number of times I would have gone home with my arms stinging from pampas grass gashes or rose thorns or plants that you can be a bit allergic to. I would go to wash my hands and really know it then when it started to sting.

Plants were posted all over England and the Channel Isles and even to the conti-

nent. British Rail used to send a lorry in every day to be loaded up with stuff that was all packed to be sent by rail all over the country. A company called Hall's used to send lorries in every day, it wasn't just local but some people did come in and pick up their orders.

Jackman's was like all the nurseries. They were all taken over by the Ministry of Agriculture during the War and told to grow a third of plants just for luxury and two thirds of the land for crops.

A dormant clematis looks like a bit of brown twiggy old string. When post packing one you'd have to be careful not to damage it. It was tied with this osier (grown in beds in a field near Smart's Heath Road) before being put in a box and packed with straw. I remember there was a complaint from a lady saying that she was disgusted and surprised to open the box to find dead twigs and old piece of plant with no roots on. Anyway knowing Jackman's reputation she planted it expecting to see a beautiful blue climber but it looked nothing more than a common osier. She had thrown away the clematis and stuck the osier in the ground! Mr Jackman used to think this was ever so funny.

Jackman's was like all the nurseries. They were all taken over by the Ministry of Agriculture during the War and told to grow a third of plants just for luxury and two thirds of the land for crops. I think it was lettuce and tomatoes in the greenhouses and a lot of the field was for root crops. Even when I started in 1962 when we rotavated the field (where you go up the hill opposite Barnsbury Estate) we kept digging up potatoes. As we kept digging them up all the time to plant it was like propagating them. One chap took them home and I can remember him saying what a lovely Sunday lunch because of these potatoes.

I was lucky that I went into the nursery business at the very tail end of the old fashioned way of doing things. Mr Rowland Jackman was the boss at the time. He was a very fair and good boss and they didn't have a particularly big turnover of staff. In the first few years that I was there they still had gentlemen there in their eighties that had worked at Jackman's all their lives and they were still out there digging, hoeing and propagating, or whatever. There must have been a dozen or more staff in the office and about thirty-six working in the nursery including ten Italians. The Italians were funny as they would use their 'budding, pruning and scraping boots knife' to open the tins of sardines and tins of tomatoes they brought for lunch to eat with their bread.

The Italians were funny as they would use their 'budding, pruning and scraping boots knife' to open the tins of sardines and tomatoes they brought for lunch to eat with their bread.

Jackman's were really noted for their clematis because they had the name from Rowland Jackman's grandfather and father for developing them and cross hybridising them. I know that the clematis, Barbara Dibley is named after Barbara Voneshen (formerly Barbara Dibley) who was Mr Jackman's secretary.

Mr Jackman sold out in 1968 to a Mr David McNeill, who knew that garden centres were going to become the 'in' thing. He gradually cut down all the growing and started containerising everything and turned it into a garden centre.

Mr Jackman sold out in 1968 to a Mr David McNeill, who knew that garden centres were going to become the 'in' thing. He gradually cut down all the growing and started containerising everything and turned it into a garden centre. Mr McNeill got this old prefab building which up until recently was Woking Lawnmowers. That was the original garden centre building. They were selling all the stuff that they'd grown like roses and I remember lots of raspberry canes. We potted all our own stuff up and one of the first things that he did was to sell off the ground where the old glasshouses were. That was where Fred Sutton sold his conifers.

Fred Sutton used to be the conifer grower and he used to love his dwarf conifers. When word got around that we were getting rid of stuff people would make offers for certain things. There were some slow growing conifers that were years old and someone paid £50 each for three of them. This is back in the late 1960s which was a lot of money then. Fred carefully dug them up and prepared them for transplanting and was very upset when the bloke collecting them cut the roots clean off. The people that had bought them were from a film company who were filming in a water tank, a 'This man from Atlantis' type film, and these conifers were the only thing that looked like real coral when they were floating in the tank.

The change into a Garden Centre happened quite quickly. Some staff took voluntary redundancy and others left. A lot of people were upset about the way it was but that was just the changing way of horticulture. I went from doing actually hands-on growing to just dealing with the public. I think if I had been working there for ten years in that old style of doing everything I probably would have been really upset. They went to buying things in from Holland, like azaleas used to come in as tiny little potted plants. It was amazing how many millions of plants you could get on a container lorry. Half the lorry was for us and half for Slocock's, or was it Waterer's. We bought the plants in rather than propagate them but potted them on before taking them down the Garden Centre. I should think by the beginning of the 1980s plants came in and nothing was done to them, they were just sold. We still had stock down the nurseries but it kept being brought up until there wasn't anything left. Then it was just a retail outlet.

David McNeill had the Garden Centre for ten years until it was sold again in 1978 to Sir Ernest Harrison. Wyevale took over in 1997.
Jackie Everett

Henry Shoesmith had a small nursery in Claremont Avenue, Woking, where he mainly dealt with dahlias. He wrote articles in the Horticultural Trades Journal. His son, my father-in-law became interested from his father and when he was released from World War 1 he – my father-in-law – took on this smallholding in Moor Lane and it went from there to grow 'Shoesmith's famous chrysanthemums'.

During the Second World War we were not exhibiting but we were producing the varieties mainly for the commercial cut flower market although this was limited because we had to grow tomatoes for the War.

During the Second World War we were not exhibiting but we were producing the varieties mainly for the commercial cut flower market although this was limited because we had to grow tomatoes for the War. The nursery was moved to a different spot in Moor Lane after my husband returned from the Second World War. We would have up to about seven people working with us. We did a lot of work ourselves.

It was from the late '40s onwards that the majority of the varieties were bred for exhibition, for the amateur exhibitor, which my husband was very keen to do. So we were then producing varieties, some for the commercial market, cut flower market, and also for exhibitors.

As we got well into the '50s, my husband, Leonard, was asked if he would produce some varieties for the year-round culture. With year-round culture, they are not natural season varieties; they are pro-

Harry (left), May and Len Shoesmith with seedlings at Shoesmith's Nursery
May Ryde

duced to become controlled under light or dark and various heats in the greenhouses, etc.. It took my husband about five years to really produce something that was going to be suitable for the England market, and once he had established his parent line, then the success came quite rapidly.

It was really when these year-round varieties were being produced by my husband, in conjunction with the company here in England that had asked him to do the work, that we had two companies in the States approach us. In 1966 we went

over and did the programmes for the American market and that proved to be very successful too. We had very good working relations with our American companies. We retained our independence the whole way producing varieties for them and in effect, our company, H. Shoesmith Ltd., is still in existence, although it's a holding company but I still own that company.

So it was very exciting then producing these new varieties for exhibitors. Then of course we did go to the exhibitions in

May Ryde (formerly Shoesmith) surrounded by chrysanthemums
May Ryde

London, taking these varieties, meeting our customers and all these wonderful varieties. We exported to America and to the continent – Holland, Belgium, Denmark etc.. Not so much to Australia but to New Zealand.

We have varieties: one that was named after an uncle of my husband's, Fred Shoesmith; one called Shoesmith Salmon, which was a most beautiful flower – pink shades, cream, salmon – and I know that some growers still grow it; another called May Shoesmith; one Prince Charles, an outdoor flowering beautiful bronze variety; and of course Princess Anne is one of the most prolific and most widely used. There are varying colours of Princess Anne now: there is a cream, a flaxen, a bronze and I think there's an amber. They're all so numerous it's impossible to mention but in all aspects of chrysanthemum growing, there are Shoesmith varieties.

My proudest moment was when the Gold Medal was awarded by the Americans to my husband posthumously and I went to Washington to receive it.

Varieties were put to the Committee of the National Chrysanthemum Society and we had First Class Certificates and Awards of Merits. My proudest moment was when the Gold Medal was awarded by the Americans to my husband posthumously and I went to Washington to receive it. It was, obviously, a very sad time too that he didn't know of the success of his work. He had partially retired in 1981 but then continued to be a consultant and go out to the States until he died in 1983.
May Ryde

My single name was Emmett. The Nursery was called Emmett and Sons and was in Kirby Road, Horsell but we lived in 1 and 3 Abbey Road. Being that we had the nursery, we never had holidays because my father would never go away. The nurseries were started by my grandfather in about 1905.

Being that we had the nursery, we never had holidays because my father would never go away.

My uncle lived in 64 Goldsworth Road (which was a big house with stables at the side). In the first instance we had a stall outside. After a couple of years, he decided to make two shops in the front. One he had for himself as an ironmongery and in the other we started our greengrocery business. We would sell our own products in the shop and had the shop from 1922 to 1976.

The nursery was run by my father who everybody knew as Mr Emmett. It ran all the way along Kirby Road and then it went at the back of Abbey Road. It was an 'L' shape. He used to grow trees, flowers, and a few vegetables. There were some lovely apple and pear trees. My father used to grow a lot of conifer trees all by hand, which other nursery people used to come and want. In them days there was a lot for box hedging. He had all kinds of rockery plants as well. There was a lot of soft fruit, we had plum trees and greengages, raspberries, so there was always something that we could sell, that would keep us going at that particular time and this lasted until the early '30s. All the other nurseries around the district used to come to my father if they wanted anything, so we used to supply everybody else –

Slocock's, Smith's, Mimbridge. In them days I think all the little nurseries used to supply each other.

We also had a piece of land which I've just remembered which was in Waldens Road, which we grew a lot of flowers on and I think there was some vegetables grown up there.

Then of course, a lot of the nursery got taken over by big greenhouses, which was for growing tomatoes in the summer, then all the staging would come down, all the Christmas stuff would go in. Part of it would be used for growing big chrysanths which people used to order; there were the cyclamen, the solanums, all the rest of the Christmas plants, which was all sold up at the shop.

Irene Brice

The men tended to stay in the business for all of their lives. I think that would have been true in any walk of life. People didn't move from one job to another.

I managed to secure a job in Chobham, with T. Hilling which was then about fifteen years old. The company went from strength to strength and I was there for twenty years – between 1930 and 1955. It ended up being three hundred and thirty acres in extent and was from Chobham right up to West End by what was Gordon Boys' Home and out to Windlesham.

When I first started it had two or three fields in Chobham and employed six or eight men for about six or ten acres, I can't remember exactly. The men tended to stay in the business for all of their lives. I think that would have been true in any walk of life. People didn't move from one job to another. They developed a skill and it was valued. Everything was worked by hand. The nursery was specialising in trees and shrubs. I was engaged to start an herbaceous and alpine department from scratch. In due course we had a very good list of plants. I gradually assumed sort of managership of the whole thing.

It was an international business. I remember we sent a lot of Christmas trees to Iceland of all places and thirty-two thousand hops to Bulgaria.

The plants were sold almost entirely wholesale. Plants were delivered by lorry – if the order was worthwhile. Woking and Bagshot stations were alive with packed trees and shrubs in enormous bales, covered with straw or hay or bracken. Some of them would be ten or twelve feet long and four feet thick. They were all packed in the nursery. We had a special packing machine which, with the aid of chains, pulleys, wheels and things, made the trees and shrubs into compact bundles so that they were easy to handle. There was no polythene in those days but after the War polythene had just become available and we used to treasure it for the despatch of small airmail parcels.

It was an international business. I re-member we sent a lot of Christmas trees to Iceland of all places and thirty-two thousand hops to Bulgaria. That was just after the War. I think the poor people out there must have been very short of beer.

Bomb damage at Hilling's Nursery, 1945
The Lightbox

Canadian soldiers helping with the harvest at Hilling's Nursery, 1946
The Lightbox

We didn't grow hops but we purchased them from Herefordshire and Kent. It was an astonishing thing.

World War II had a big effect on the nursery. We became farmers on the Government's instruction. All nurseries were allowed to keep a nucleus of stock, a few stock plants or just something so that the stock wasn't lost. We had some of the very best wheat land in the country, I was told. We grew acres of winter lettuce. They were planted out in October and spent the winter out of doors and all of a sudden grew nicely in the spring and were marketed. We had four one-hundred-foot-long greenhouses which were almost entirely given over to tomatoes and a few cucumbers and we grew onions and carrots. We needed an expansion in the labour force to do all that and to supplement the lack of men we had landgirls and a number of local women.

We had two sheds blown up in one night, with the fire bombs. We had a doodlebug later.

The produce was always sold by what was called 'an arrangement'. There were market gardeners in the district. Of course it was quite a bulky business, I mean a thousand lettuces at a time or something like that, take up a bit of space, but we were not big enough to get in touch with the substitute for Covent Garden in those days. So we were very glad to have an outlet, a big market gardener just the other side of Chobham.

We had two sheds blown up in one night, with the fire bombs. We had a doodlebug later. We had to fire watch our offices which were in Chobham because it was that kind of building which was often

Everybody during the War wanted to buy fruit trees and there was a huge overstock at the end of it because people suddenly stopped buying them.

bombed. Fire watching was very exhausting; you didn't feel like work the next day.

After the War it was still operated as a wholesale nursery. There was a tremendous demand for ornamental stock. We had been very much geared to fruit tree production. Everybody during the War wanted to buy fruit trees and there was a huge overstock at the end of it because people suddenly stopped buying them. Many were dumped.

At the end of the War, we were able to purchase some small cultivating machines, about as big as a large lawn mower which, of course, made a huge difference to the quelling of weeds between the rows and the ploughs were used for the beds and borders, instead of hand digging.

Tom Hilling had no descendants and he sold the business to a firm who had been our accountants for many years. The son of the accountant gradually sold off the whole shoot. I believe there's an acre of land somewhere down at Haslemere which is called Hilling & Co. and that's all there is left.
Graham Thomas

Prisoners of War worked in the nursery grounds and also on McBey's Farm which was down Smart's Heath Road. (There's a turning off to the left that goes to Kemishford, but right opposite that where now they keep ponies was old McBey's Farm.) He had Prisoners of War there in Nissen huts working on the farm. But they were real nice men. They were Italian and I was allowed to talk to them. It was the German ones I had to be a bit wary with at the time. It sounds ridiculous now but that's the way we thought. They used to get jobs clearing out the Hoe Stream and all the ditches and things and they liked it, because it passed the time for them and we liked it because it kept our riverbanks nice and clean and tidy. Right through the War, and obviously before, the cattle were driven down the road. They used to come out from Loampits Farm and plod at their normal plodding speed round the corner by the cycle shop and the forge, down the hill, and then one of the chaps would stand in the road directing them into the lower meadows down by the Hoe Stream because in the summer, the grass was short and there used to be nice, lush grass down there for the cattle. They would then be taken back again for milking so this routine used to go on every day. In fact, that's why you had to have gates on your gardens down Westfield Road because you'd end up with a dairy cow in your front drive. The thing you got used to was the cattle deposits in the road, especially if you were riding bikes, not to be a bit too unobservant otherwise you'd end up in trouble.
John Noble

I did two paper rounds before school, did gardening jobs, did a butcher's delivery, I did anything and did my own garden at home. If I had two or three pence that was plenty in those days.

My earliest memories are probably before I started school and I started school before I was five years old. I was on the farm, in Byfleet. My father milked cows and I would spend a lot of time on the farm with him. My father went to work every day because, in those days, on farms, you didn't have a day off. We lived a much simpler life in those days. We had sheep, cattle, pigs and chicken – it was a mixed farm, as most of the farms were then.

I did two paper rounds before school, did gardening jobs, did a butcher's delivery, I did anything and did my own garden at home. If I had two or three pence that was plenty in those days, you'd buy plenty of sweets for tuppence, which is one new pence or thereabouts these days.

During the War it was easier being on the farm because you'd get eggs for a start, you wouldn't get any more meat. On the farm we could get some extra eggs as they were rationed as well. You could get corn (from the farm) and we always had our own chicken at home. You could fatten a chicken up and eat that. At Christmas we used to have a goose, because where I lived there was an old pond out the back and we kept a few geese.
Geoffrey Simpson

There seemed to be a lot of go-slows, working to rule or straightforward strikes disrupting travel more than now.

They were all dressed in dark grey suits and black shiny shoes and white shirts and bowler hats and quite often, they'd have an umbrella and a rolled newspaper under their arm – and they all looked the same.

Steam trains were great because they were on time to the second. It didn't matter whether it was ice or leaves or whatever it was, they just went belting on.

Well, if it wasn't for the railway, Woking would be a very different place.

4. The Railway and Commuting

Well, if it wasn't for the railway, Woking would be a very different place.
In 1838, when they decided to make a line from London to Southampton, they surveyed it across something called Woking Common, which was a genuine bit of Surrey Heath and there was Woking village on one side and Horsell village on the other, and it went through the middle, and there was nothing there before that. It was the railway that created it and without it, goodness knows what it would have been like – probably still a bit of blasted heath. It obviously produced jobs, it produced a centre.
John Davenport

Well, if it wasn't for the railway, Woking would be a very different place.

My father was a plate layer on the railway. He used to work along the line from Woking to Brookwood. I remember him going out 'fogging', when they put little devices on the line so that the train driver would know where they were. Fogging lights. And I used to be so afraid because he used to go out on a sit-up-and-beg-bike, with his bottle of cold tea, which would have got cold by the time he drank it and his few sandwiches. And they had a little, what they called the 'Fogging Hut', on the edge of the line from Woking to Brookwood. Then they'd stay there all night and they'd go and put these detonators (I think they were called) on the line and other times he'd just work with his mates laying sleepers and whatever they do on the railway.
Gladys Newlyn

I remember him going out 'fogging', when they put little devices on the line so that the train driver would know where they were.

This was the fastest station, it was remarkable and it was in good trim then and on time, always.
Katharine Buchanan

The reason we chose this area was precisely because of Woking railway station. Woking station stood out for its superb railway service, so it was frequency of trains that made us decide to look for a house in a village within a few miles of Woking.
Guy Consterdine

A friend of mine in those days who I went to school with, her father was the signalman, signal box man. So she used to come sometimes and call for me and says, 'Do you want to come down to take my dad's lunch?' and it would be a little pack of sandwiches and a billycan of tea. The tea was cold by the time you got it there. We walked down this little bit of path – it wasn't far into what's Sheerwater now – and when we got to this place I think there was a little gate and some steps took you up to his signal box and we used to go in. It would be only him in there and he'd got all these levers and when the trains were coming, to stop them or start them or make them go slower, they pulled the levers.
Betty Curtis

Oriental Road was like a country lane, and there were no houses apart from one on the railway side, and the one house was Rastrick's. He must have been a funny old chap, died long before we were there. In fact, when I was going to the Grammar School we used to call this old house 'the spooky house' because all the windows were broken and that sort of thing. And this old chap was really the cause of Woking town getting sandwiched between the railway and the canal. They brought the railway to Woking, and then they built the front part of the station on the south side of Woking.

This old chap owned quite a bit of land around there, and he wouldn't sell, and there was no compulsory purchase in those days, so that's why the town developed on the other side. I can remember there was a high brick wall where the shops are in Oriental Road at the top, before they were built of course, and there was a little lodge behind this wall. The wall had a slab in it, oblong it was, and it had Rastrick's name written backwards! Another thing that a lot of people probably don't know and I haven't had it checked out, but there was an underground tunnel from his place. The brother's house, I believe, was opposite the station, where a telephone exchange used to be. I have seen the entrance, but not many people seem to know about it.
Joan Roberts

Rastrick's commemorative plaque; his name written backwards is thought to be symbolic of his disapproval of the railway and turning his back on Woking *The Lightbox*

Looking down the platforms, 1961
South Western Circle

Southern Railway Orphanage, Woking c.1912
The Lightbox

I discovered what Woking was like when I began commuting. Essentially it was a superb railway service with a railway station whose entrance that I was using, from the town side, was a surprisingly small pokey little entrance, because in a sense the main booking hall had been built on the wrong side of the railway in relation to the way the town developed.

The station itself has changed quite a lot. In 1966, when I started commuting, there was a platform where the bus bay is now and that was platform 1. What is now platform 1 was platform 2, and what's now platform 2 was platform 3 and there was no platform at the Waterloo end of the platform as there is now, which is now called platform 3 – that didn't exist. When they filled in platform 1 and built the wall and the bus station on the other side of it, it was some while before they renumbered the platforms, but eventually they did renumber them so that it started at 1.

It's much better now. There is more space; it's lighter and brighter and more modern and efficient. It doesn't look like the back end of something so much, which it definitely did before.
Guy Consterdine

The lady who lived next door to me was a Mrs Aylesbury who had three children at the Railway Orphanage. Her husband got killed on the railway. In those days, you didn't have a paper towel, but you had an ordinary towel marked 'Southern Railway' and she used to wash hundreds of these, and I mean hundreds a week and she used to get her money by washing the towels for the Southern Railway.
Philip Ledger

One of the fun things that we've lost is a lot of advertising on enamel sheets.

The railways have developed over the years and so have the railway servants, as they were so often called, meaning the guard, the driver, porters, station staff. They all had more or less a uniform material, sort of heavyweight blue serge was the standard railway issue, but they were very hard-wearing clothes. I had some when I was working in the steam locomotive maintenance depots, and super-waterproof raincoats that we were issued with.

One of the fun things that we've lost is a lot of advertising on enamel sheets. The one I remember particularly was for cocoa – don't ask me whose cocoa – but somebody's cocoa. I remember this and I think there were also early Coca Cola adverts as well.
John Mitchell

I don't know whether I should say this but we used to go on the train at Woking Station and in those days you had a platform ticket, so we would get on the train at Woking with a platform ticket. We'd get off at Wimbledon South, I think it was, and we'd go up to the gate and we'd pay from Raynes Park. Because we'd say there was no one on the gate at Raynes Park. And one particular day we said this and then the porter said, 'Well, hang on a minute. This train didn't stop at Raynes Park.' And that's when we thought, well, we better change this now. And the following week we went up and we paid the proper fare and there must have been three or four policeman at the gate, waiting to see.
Richard Wooller

I had a car park season ticket and I parked in the forecourt where there's now the short term parking and then they decided that we should move out of there. So they demolished what was the stationmaster's house and put us up on the car park that is now just behind the forecourt. They had a chap, he was semi-retired, and his only job was in the morning to make sure that only his regulars got into their spaces in the car park and no interlopers got in, because there were that many tickets, season ticket holders for the number of spaces. There were no spare, so he had a terrible job if somebody sneaked in when he wasn't looking. He always found somewhere for his regulars to go somehow – I'm not quite sure how.

Travelling ticket collectors were a very rare breed. If it was the normal ticket collector, he knew who you were. Quite often you were going through at a gallop anyway because you were late and the train was coming, but you just took it out of your pocket and just waved something at him and said, 'Morning' and if he knew you, it was fine. Sometimes they would put ticket inspectors on the entrance, because there were no barriers, it was just an entrance and then you actually had to show your ticket.

Tickets were in racks on the wall with all the destinations: first class, second class, dogs, bicycles, children – whatever – and as you took one out, the next one was just projecting. White was first class and green was second or third.
John Davenport

Tickets were in racks on the wall with all the destinations: first class, second class, dogs, bicycles, children.

The main entrance to Woking Railway Station, c.1960 *The Lightbox*

In my teenage years we used to travel from Walton to West Byfleet by train and stopped to meet up with friends at West Byfleet. Then we'd get back on the train and travel to Woking, and we would go to a disco in a place called 'The Albion' but it's been knocked down years and years ago now. I hadn't got a clue then where Woking was at all. All I knew was that you got on the train at Walton and a few stops later you got off and it was where this disco was. But I could have been anywhere.
Elizabeth Seward

They had a chap, he was semi-retired, and his only job was in the morning to make sure that only his regulars got into their spaces in the car park and no interlopers got in.

Staff had 'SR' (Southern Railway) on their lapels, on their caps, or on a badge on their caps. You could tell who was a railway worker, they were dressed properly. Drivers had what's called a 'grease-top' hat, which is a cap with a waterproof, greaseproof covering on the top, and blue overalls, a jacket and dungarees, because they always got dirty. The fireman was the one who used to get the dirtiest.

One or two drivers believed in going as fast as they could, particularly driving the Portsmouth electrics.

One or two drivers believed in going as fast as they could, particularly driving the Portsmouth electrics, which did sway and rattle and bump a bit and one or two of those drivers, they thought they wanted to see how fast they could get to Woking.

You had the stationmaster and you had the inspectors, who were basically in charge of the platforms. Then you had the porters, whose jobs were really to get people on and off the trains, wave to the guard when everything was ready, sweep the platforms, and keep the place tidy, help with the luggage. There were loads of parcels and things floating round, as there were whole trains of parcels which used to come in and unload and load up. That all had to be dealt with by the station staff with barrows and all sorts of things.

There were always meant to be porters to carry your luggage, particularly before the lift was built. The old subway that now goes underneath the station used to be the way up to the platforms. There was a slope up from underneath, up onto each platform, so there were a lot of people around to actually 'hoick' your luggage around for you on a barrow or carry it. The Stationmaster was pretty well always visible, particularly during the rush hour when it was important that the trains tried to behave themselves! The passengers got on and off without any problems and everything went efficiently. He was usually there as a presence, just to show that he cared. He had a special uniform and a hat with brass edges. You could tell he was a stationmaster.

Because my father was commuting throughout the War, he knew the Stationmaster very well. I got up into the Woking signal box with some friends and we had a guided tour. It was great fun because it was modern and the levers were tiny and it had lots of coloured lights and all sorts of interesting things.

The Stationmaster in the War was Mr Winifrith and the one I knew best was Mr Piper.

The station used to have W H Smiths bookstall, on platform 1. I think it had the equivalent of a refreshment room on platform 1 and on the middle platform as well.

Woking was civilised. It had a loudspeaker system which was operated from the signal box for many years by a chap who was partially disabled and he was very good. Always the announcement would come just as a train went through. If you knew what the chap was saying, you could understand it because he would be saying that this train stopped at wherever it was and if you knew what the train was anyway, you didn't need to worry. I think sometimes they weren't very clear to people who didn't know. You did get people on the station saying, 'What did he say?' We had classic examples of, 'The next train to arrive at your platform will be...' whatever it was, and it would go hurtling through at 90 miles an hour blowing its whistle like mad and after that, you would get, 'I do apologise' or something like that. The trains weren't wired for sound at all. The only time you got announcements was when there was a serious problem and the guard would eventually find out what it was and he would have to go and tell everybody – if he could get through the train, depending on how full of bodies it was.

Every so often, there would appear this very smart train of three or four coaches and sometimes it even had a Pullman car in it and a clean engine, which in wartime was almost unheard of. It would come really quite fast round through Woking and as we didn't know what it was and it was so extraordinary, we called it the 'Hush-hush special', because you had no idea what was going on. In fact, it was the train to and from Poole where the British Overseas Airways flying boats were taking off and landing and it used to bring the passengers from that up to Victoria.
John Davenport

Woking was civilised. It had a loud-speaker system which was operated from the signal box for many years by a chap who was partially disabled and he was very good.

The re-building of Woking Station, 1920s
Lens of Sutton

A suburban electric train at Woking station, 1960 *Lens of Sutton*

I remember there was a special train that went down to Devon and at the end, the back of the train, it had got windows all round so that you could sit in. It was like a glasshouse so that you could see all the scenery on your way down to Devon.

I remember there was a special train that went down to Devon and at the end, the back of the train, it had got windows all round so that you could sit in. It was like a glasshouse so that you could see all the scenery on your way down to Devon. Because we were so near the station, we've always used trains. If you went to London shopping, if you got out and caught the 7.06 train from Woking, you got a workman's ticket to Weybridge, you got out at Weybridge, went up the steps, got another ticket to Waterloo in time to come down the steps and catch the next train to Waterloo. By that, we got a workman's ticket and I think we got to London for about 1/7d, but you had to be bothered to do that.
Emily Gloster

My father, who was very keen on cricket, would take us up to the Oval at Kennington. The thing was that we could walk to Woking Railway Station, and providing we took a train before I think about 7am, we could buy what was called a workman's ticket for a very small sum. That would take us up to Vauxhall station, just outside Waterloo, and we'd get off there and walk down to the Oval.
William Ledger

A lot of commuters wore bowler hats, rolled umbrellas, the rest of it – proper job – not like the way they go to work these days. I wore a suit, in the summer a dress – tidy. I was working in an art gallery in Bond Street.
Margaret Eatough

I never wore a hat but we did expect to go to work in a dark business suit, tie and we always wore a raincoat.
John Mitchell

I can remember before the War, my uncle and a whole crowd of others, it was all black coat and striped trousers and you all had high collars. I was the same when I first started off, all detachable linen collars, starched. That was the sort of formal dress until certainly the late '50s and the odd one would appear with a collar-attached shirt and then the floodgate opened and that was the end of it.
Derek Haycroft

As we got nearer to the station, we used to notice these people coming out of the houses and the side roads leading into White Rose Lane and they all looked the same. They were all dressed in dark grey suits and black shiny shoes and white shirts and bowler hats and quite often, they'd have an umbrella and a rolled newspaper under their arm – and they all looked the same. They were going into the station and when we got to the top of the hill – where the sorting office is now – they'd be swarming in and they'd be pushing and shoving and they wouldn't speak to each other.
Jennifer Wharam

It was steam trains when I first went. I went up to Waterloo, and I walked over Waterloo Bridge to Fleet Street. The trains weren't that crowded, you nearly always got a seat, and as usual, most people in those days, business people, had a paper and would bury their heads in the paper, and you didn't get a lot of conversation. If you did start to talk, people didn't like it.
Joan Roberts

They were all dressed in dark grey suits and black shiny shoes and white shirts and bowler hats and quite often, they'd have an umbrella and a rolled newspaper under their arm – and they all looked the same.

We used to have orange curtains which we could draw to and fro but they all went very quickly, from probably being vandalised, but that was commuting. It was not really that horrible. You just get used to it and, mainly, the problems are about the size of the fare and the sort of lack of information about mysterious reasons for lateness. I knew one once that it took about two hours to get home. What did we do when we were commuting? Read one way, possibly sleep. There used to be many more strikes and we all crammed in together. I found myself crammed next to somebody. I was reading Dr. Zhivago and he was, I think, reading Solzhenitsyn. We sort of looked at each other and were thinking this is the sort of hell which we might get if it carries on like this. There's this enormous great train ride in Dr. Zhivago, where they go for days in this box van and people were sort of being pretty awful at the time. Well, it was getting a bit like that at times – just getting extremely squashed.

There was the bucket in the guard's van. You could always sit on the bucket because they had these plates which came on the front of the train to give them numbers. These were loose plates and, if you didn't mind the shape of an '8' impressed on your bottom, it was not too bad. The '8' was the train code, you see. They had all these loose numbers on big slats which were metal. You could put these on top of the bucket and sit down. Some more expert commuters used to have their shooting sticks and folding stools and things to sit on.

You could always sit on the bucket because they had these plates which came on the front of the train to give them numbers. These were loose plates and, if you didn't mind the shape of an '8' impressed on your bottom, it was not too bad.

You don't talk to people on the train, I mean, even if you were to know them. Mostly we buried ourselves in our newspapers. You can see the same people at other times and talk to them socially. Now, of course, the most noise is people talking on their mobiles. If someone spoke, we'd say, 'Hello' – if we actually looked up from the paper to see who they were. We had a dreadful man from Walton-on-Thames who we always avoided. Though he was pure English he had developed the total look of an Orangeman and the accents of Northern Ireland Protestant and used to go to all these sorts of rallies and things for the Ulster Unionists and whatever, you know? He always had snuff all over his waistcoat and used to wear a bowler hat after everybody else had stopped doing it. Quite often, he was boring and noisy.
Richard Christophers

It was easy because there was always a seat on the train. There wasn't all this hassle that there is now – you could park, you could drop your bike anywhere. There weren't so many people – there wasn't the pressure on everything, whereas now it's all pushing and shoving and nobody's got a minute. Commuting was easy. The trains were on time, they were clean, they were on the dot and there was always a seat. I met my husband because he was commuting as well and he kept on saying, 'Would you like a lift?' and I'd keep on saying, 'I've got my bike thank you.'
Wendy Davenport

My father was a commuter in the late 1950s, early '60s and he got offered a job in London at the same time that I was going to start grammar school, and we worked out that his train and my bus would leave Woking station about the same time. So we decided to walk up to the station together in the mornings and we'd walk up to the station along White Rose Lane. My father and I would go under the subway and we would end up at the town side of the station and he used to go and get his train, which left from platform 3. I'd go and get my bus, and walking towards the bus stop I would pass a stone wall. Above it was a poster board and in between the wall and the poster board was a slit and if I stood on tiptoe and I looked through, I could actually see my father on the platform. When I told him about this he said, 'I'll stand in a special place so that I can see you.' So every morning I'd look through the slit and I'd wave at him and he'd wave back. Then the train would come in and it was a wonderful steam train. The guard would close the doors and then all of a sudden, you'd hear the train go. I really loved the steam trains. They had a magic and a beauty about

I really loved the steam trains. They had a magic and a beauty about them that unfortunately environmentally friendly modern trains don't have.

them that unfortunately environmentally friendly modern trains don't have, and I always used to think my dad had an exciting trip to London and I had to just get on my bus to go to school. He used to hate the journeys in the winter because people wanted the windows closed. They would be steaming with all the condensation and everything and people would be coughing and sneezing.

I think it was a part of his life that he really enjoyed and I don't think the trains were ever late or anything, maybe a couple of minutes. I think it was twenty-eight minutes it took for this train to get to Waterloo.
Jennifer Wharam

The trains to London were quite reliable and punctual. There was the odd time when they were a bit late, but it didn't really matter too much because there were lots of trains from Woking. I really quite enjoyed commuting to London. It was only half an hour and I really quite enjoyed it, reading a book. I didn't feel at all frustrated and stressed. It was probably partly because, when I got to Waterloo, it was only a short walk to the office in Holborn.
Roger Thomas

Steam trains were great because they were on time to the second. It didn't matter whether it was ice or leaves or whatever it was, they just went belting on.

I started at 6 at night and finished at 2 in the morning – so I used to get the 2.30 milk train. I had a special pass on the 2.30 milk train which didn't officially stop at Woking but did to put the milk off and the newspapers.
David Evans

Steam trains were great because they were on time to the second. It didn't matter whether it was ice or leaves or whatever it was, they just went belting on and there was something really quite nice about them. The electric – because the Southern had electrified at quite an early date – were quite good and efficient, but gave a jerky ride, whereas the steamer, once it started to pull, was just gliding along. They got up an amazing turn of speed when they got going. It was quite an evocative thing, the smell of hot oil and steam.

People would thank the engine driver as they walked past him too, because he was still standing there wiping his hands on a bit of cotton waste and watching everybody – quite nice really.
Derek Haycroft

Away from the War, it was rather fun because I got in at Fleet and I had a friend who got in at the next station at Farnborough. We used to bring our embroidery to do on the train, but we didn't want all the Woking people in the carriage. So when the train got to Woking, we used to stand at the doorway as if we were waiting for somebody and that meant we kept it empty to London. When I started commuting from Woking I was one who tried to get in. I found it a lot different – much easier because from Woking, the train didn't stop till Waterloo. It got me home a lot earlier, but of course, I didn't come in to a meal, I had to come in and get one.
Serena Whiteman

I had a special pass on the 2.30 milk train which didn't officially stop at Woking but did to put the milk off and the newspapers.

One of the main benefits of travelling by train was the privacy. It was the one time of the day when you had it entirely to yourself and I would read, but the essential thing was, although you're surrounded by masses of people and sometimes standing – but even if sitting in the rush hour, often you had people standing around you – in another sense, I was very much on my own and all of us were, there wasn't usually a lot of talking. So it was a valuable contrast to life at home which was very happy but always with other people, my wife and children, and at work, masses of people. This was the one time while travelling on the train that I could be on my own for an extended period.
Guy Consterdine

Woking Station façade, 1970s *Woking History Society*

Woking Junction Station, with a 'Greyhound' engine, c.1913 *Lens of Sutton*

People would thank the engine driver as they walked past him too, because he was still standing there wiping his hands on a bit of cotton waste.

I suppose one notable thing is that when I moved in April '67, for the first three months I used to go up on a steam train. There were just a few steam trains still on the line beyond Brookwood, and a few of the steam trains didn't stop at Woking. This one in the morning did. Steam trains used to have some ropey old carriages on them and they were really rather dirty and bitty but they looked very romantic.
Richard Christophers

Well, commuting is not all a dead loss. People talk about it being a dead loss as though it's a nuisance, an inconvenience and so on. Well, it is and it isn't. At least it gives you the opportunity of something like thirty to forty minutes of each day of, in some respects, relative peace that you can read the local papers or the daily papers or, indeed, read your technical magazine, which leaves you time when you get home to do other things as well.

On the whole we think the trains were fairly good at timekeeping – in fact in many ways better timekeeping than in more recent years.
John Mitchell

The locomotive itself, with all the steam and hissing noise, was like a live animal.

The habit of hiding behind the newspaper is not a modern one. Some people chatted, most people read the paper or worked or whatever. It was only when coming home in my younger days, with the rowdy mob of young people who had the compartment to themselves, when nobody was trying to read a paper, but generally no, it was all quiet.

It was total boredom and if you did it often enough, you knew exactly where the train was in its journey without looking out of the window. So you never had to look out, you knew that you were just past somewhere or you were just about to get to something and you got this sort of sense that you had done so much and the train had just gone over a set of points or round a curve. You just knew. I used to look out at Clapham because you never knew what odd engines or trains you might see. Normally it was heads down in the paper.

It was total boredom and if you did it often enough, you knew exactly where the train was in its journey without looking out of the window.

You got in the train, you sat down, and you read your paper because you'd got to. Or coming home, you were reading something else or thinking about whatever. When it was a steam train, there was always something, you were always listening to it or thinking how fast it was going or whatever.
John Davenport

One of the trains I used to catch was the 8.44 and I particularly liked that one because it was a steam train. When I arrived here, at the very end of 1965, we knew that the steam trains were going to be withdrawn later that year, and it was only a few services that the steam trains were operating on. Mostly it was electric trains and diesels were coming in. But I liked the steam trains, partly for nostalgic reasons, so if there was one at a convenient time out of two or three trains, then I'd catch the steam one if I could. Nowadays they're air conditioned for one thing, which is a huge advance. When I was commuting every day in the late '60s and the first half of the '70s, in the summer on a hot day everyone in the carriage, even with the windows down, would be sweltering and sticky and it could be very unpleasant. It's such a boon to have air-conditioned travelling and the whole experience of the actual journey is so much better. Another difference is the continuous track. You got the 'clickety-click, clickety-click, clickety-click' noise all the time as the train went over all these joins of the rail and now that it's long, long stretches of one continuous rail it's quieter and there isn't that sound. On the old rolling stock, as they pick up speed, they can rattle about and throw you about and if you're trying to write something, you can't write in proper handwriting because the pen is jagging across the paper so much.

The locomotive itself, with all the steam and hissing noise, was like a live animal and riding in the coach behind it, it would start off from the station with a series of tugs. It wasn't a smooth moving away as you have today, it was tugs and jerks and sometimes there was wheel slip. The wheels of the locomotive actually spin round, through not getting a good enough grip on the rail in wet conditions particularly, and then there was the distinctive and rather a nice smell of the smoke that would drift in through the window. Little black smuts might get in your eyes and very often on the platform end at Waterloo, there would be a number of boy train spotters or occasionally a few adults taking the numbers and taking photographs.
Guy Consterdine

LSWR locomotive at Woking 150 Exhibition, 1988
Graham Cartland Glover

To some people, I think, the bar was the main purpose of travelling. You could get in, licensing hours didn't apply on a train.

When I first started commuting up to London, we had some rolling stock which I recollect had got very plush deep cushions which you sank into when you sat down, always assuming of course that you've got a seat! Then we had the electric multiple units of two cars each and both cars had a lavatory facility. They were really very comfortable trains, and I was quite happy to travel in those.

I quite looked forward to it, having good rolling stock with nice deep plump cushions that you sank into, really very comfortable. They only had four seats a side and a side corridor, none of this central corridor business which came in in the 1960s.
John Mitchell

I used to get the 7.50 from Woking Station and this damn great steamer came in, the 'Lord Nelson' – they were all Lord something or other, that particular lot. The card players got in the last carriage and nobody would get in these last two compartments because they got in there and would say, 'Your deal Reg' and out came the cards. They finished up standing up in the guard's van in the 1950s as everybody started packing back in again. It was all very sociable then. Terrible clapped out rolling stock, as you can imagine after being thrashed by the War.
Derek Haycroft

There seemed to be a lot of go-slows, working to rule or straightforward strikes disrupting travel more than now.

When they played bridge on this train, they would almost certainly try to get this little group of them with little groups of four. On the old Portsmouth train you could take the basic cushions up. Then they would balance these on their knees so they'd have a table to play on, because it was very rare to actually get the table, they were kept in the guard's van. You never see people playing cards on a train, well not very often now. Mind you, the commuters are mostly on their mobiles or their laptops and taking no notice of the sign saying, 'No mobiles.' But over the years the trains have improved a little bit, I think.
Richard Christophers

There was very little eating on the train – after all, our entire journey was only thirty-five minutes or so. There was a buffet car or dining car on it, but it didn't really apply in the commuting stage.
John Mitchell

To some people, I think, the bar was the main purpose of travelling. You could get in, licensing hours didn't apply on a train and, sometimes, the people in the Guildford days would be all a bit worse for wear at Guildford, I think.
Richard Christophers

My father-in-law went to the Metropolitan Police every day all his life with my uncle, who was in the Foreign Office, and a Mr Sarvis, who was in the Home Office, and a Mr Norless, who was in the insurance of the Metropolitan Police and the Home Office. They all travelled together in the first class carriage and went up town together every morning, met at Woking station, and had a first class carriage reserved for them. They all got in, the door was slammed and locked and they got out their chessboards and they smoked all the way up to London. They were all smokers and I don't know what the people used to think while the train was standing there. No one would ever want to go in with them anyway because the place was filled with smoke, and the same thing happened every night. The four of them travelled down to Woking all together with their chessboard.
Peggy Battie

There seemed to be a lot of go-slows, working to rule or straightforward strikes disrupting travel more than now. I think if people are concerned about industrial disputes causing delays now, they need to go back to the 1960s and see how much more prevalent it was. Depending on how severe the disruption was, it meant you took longer but also you got frustrated. It wasn't just the time, you didn't know how long the journey was going to take and if you'd get a seat. As and when a train came in, you wondered whether it would do the journey once you started in the normal time – that really could get quite frustrating. So it wasn't just the loss of time.

The card players got in the last carriage and nobody would get in these last two compartments because they got in there and would say, 'Your deal Reg' and out came the cards.

I do remember once coming down from Waterloo to Woking and the only other person in the compartment was sitting opposite me. He had a bag in the luggage rack above him and there was some reason why I spoke to him. Normally you don't speak to your fellow passenge but something or other happened, I can't remember what it was, but I spoke to him and he replied in an extremely thick southern Irish accent. There were IRA bombings going on at that time and I was just struck by this man's accent. He clearly was from southern Ireland and he didn't want to speak. When I said something to him – he gave as short as possible answer – he didn't really want to engage in conversation. I got off the train at Woking wondering if he was anything to do with the IRA. Then a few days later – this was a train going to Southampton I should add – a few days later, there was a public revelation that there was a big IRA cell in Southampton and I've always wondered whether he was part of it.

I went in the loft and dug out my 1967 pocket diary and one or two others. On 10th July 1967, 'new BR timetable, chaos in the evening'. 28th November 1967, 'a train derailed at Raynes Park blocking all the lines, morning chaos, 9am train from Woking got to Waterloo via Chertsey at 11.05.'
Guy Consterdine

At the start, when they introduced the electrics it was an absolute shambles. It was unbelievable for the first few days as they really had no idea what they were doing. All of a sudden one Monday morning, bingo, off we go – and the trouble was, we didn't and it was an absolute lottery as to what train you got on. Hopefully they were all going to Waterloo but beyond that, it was indescribable chaos.

Privatisation produced even more trains than were running before. Not just in the rush hour but throughout the day, which was a great improvement, I think and also, there was a certain amount of sense that got into things. Clapham Junction was a station to which, if you wanted to get from Woking, you had a major job. You had to change at Surbiton or you had to go up to Waterloo and go back and nothing stopped there, which was ridiculous. Now, if you want to go to Victoria or indeed down to Brighton or the south coast or anything, you go to Clapham and hop over and that is one of the best pieces of sensible thinking that's come.

The Necropolis Line's gone. There was another one from Brookwood on the other side which ran to Bisley Camp. When the National Rifle Association meetings were on, they used to run little trains up there. During the First World War, the line was extended quite considerably into the other camps round Deepcut and out that way. Woking had an engine shed at one time – that's gone. Otherwise it's very much as it was.

John Davenport

The great freeze-up of 1962/63, that was the most incredible travelling time, because with all the snow and the ice, the electric trains couldn't pick up the current. So they had to have extra steam trains, or even sometimes steam trains attached to the electric trains. Then you had the awful problem with the steam trains that, if they were delayed, they were liable to run short of water and the water columns, from which they would get their water to fill up the tender, had frozen up. So there was the odd panic every so often – get the fire brigade out to fill up this engine and then find the hydrant was frozen as well and sometimes they had to throw the fire out before the thing got too hot. I remember being at Waterloo one evening, about 5.30pm, and there was nothing moving at all but because of my railway connections, I could find someone to ask what was happening. The chap said cheerfully, 'There are no trains moving between Clapham Junction and Waterloo and we don't know when there will be one,' and this was in the middle of the rush hour. The place was getting fuller and fuller, and it was a bit of a mess. We all got home eventually.

The great freeze-up of 1962/63, that was the most incredible travelling time, because with all the snow and the ice, the electric trains couldn't pick up the current. So they had to have extra steam trains, or even sometimes steam trains attached to the electric trains.

When we had steam trains, there were never any trees of any size. They were either burnt off gently by the steam trains setting up little fires, or they were kept clean by the people who removed anything that looked as if it might get too big.

There was a very interesting day when the bridge with the signal box on at Clapham Junction, the legs gave way and that blocked all the lines. We only ever got as far as Wimbledon and we were meant to get into Waterloo at 9.15. We eventually got thrown out at Wimbledon at 11.30 and we got the underground from Wimbledon, so it wasn't too bad. But coming back again, the people I used to travel with, we took evasive action and we came home from Paddington to Windsor and got someone to pick us up. So we cheated a bit on that one. There was a nasty accident outside the Lion Works in about 1945, when one train went into the back of another in the evening, because someone had misread the signals. Also in about 1945, there was a potentially disastrous derailment at West Byfleet, when an express train going towards London just totally came off the track. The track was in a shocking state because it hadn't been maintained properly during the War. The ballast was all clogged up and it had been raining and the engine and all the coaches came off, but by some miracle, they all stayed upright – and that was quite a mess.

When we had steam trains, there were never any trees of any size. They were either burnt off gently by the steam trains setting up little fires, or they were kept clean by the people who removed anything that looked as if it might get too big. Yes, there were one or two quite spectacular fires. One started up just by the bridge on the embankment. It did the fence no end of good, when it was a wooden fence. You could tell from the coach where the emergency cord had been pulled. There was a little indicator. This was a little flag on the outside of the coach at the corner and if someone had pulled the cord, it went up. So that you could tell exactly where it was and they would appear and say, 'Now what's all this here and who did that and what for?'

In this part of the world all the coal came in by train. There was a lot of livestock carried around and every sort of parcels and merchandise you can think of. The nurseries in Woking used to send an enormous number of their plants off by train. You'd see great loads of trees and shrubs all wrapped up at the station ready to be sent off. Milk used to go up to London from the West Country in tank wagons. Almost everything you could think of trundled around on the rail.

A very important part of Woking traffic was the post. The sorting office dealt with all the mail for Hampshire, which came from various directions and was sent on into Hampshire from Woking. But the main thing was there were mailbags whizzing around all during the day. They used to come down on little trolleys onto the platforms, but the main thing was the Weymouth-Dorchester mail at night. That was a real mail train and the platforms were absolutely stuffed, lined with these trucks full of mailbags. It was a wonderful train because it took passengers, but it also had the Royal Mail sorting carriages on it and it had a posting box in the side. If you put an extra penny stamp on your letter, you could post it in the travelling post office

and it would be sorted and dealt with. You could trundle down to the station at 11pm and post your letter knowing it would get there the next morning without any fail. I remember that you could tell at night when the mail train was going past, because you could hear the engine working like mad. Actually the house would vibrate from the noise and the effort and it was quite fun and a bit romantic in a way.
John Davenport

It also had the Royal Mail sorting carriages on it and it had a posting box in the side. If you put an extra penny stamp on your letter, you could post it in the travelling post office and it would be sorted and dealt with.

Post bags on Woking Station platform, 1960s
South Western Circle

You still had 'clickety click, clickety click' as the train went over the rails and the joint.

One of the problems of travel is always the weather and of course I was lucky from the commuting point of view that the fog that we used to get, the pea soupers, the London pea soupers, the last of those was 1952. We didn't seem to worry about having the wrong type of snow but it was always wet. The summer could be a bit hot in trains but the real problem was the track passed a number of sewage disposal plants and so you had terrible smells at certain places. I remember Berrylands was one and Weybridge had its own problem too.

We never really doubted safety with railways in those days as we do since Paddington and Hatfield. We don't seem to have worried about safety as we as-sumed that we were going to get there safely, although of course there have been some terrible accidents. More recently, of course, we've had Clapham Junction. But we still think of them being safe, trains, even commuter trains.

Nowadays of course they are all welded into six hundred foot lengths of track so as to reduce the number of 'clickety clicks'.

There were inevitably hold-ups on some days. One notable day which I remember created a lot of confusion and people didn't really know what was happening. They had a fire in a major signal box which spanned all the tracks just between Clapham Junction and Waterloo and all the trains were turned and reversed at Wimbledon. Fortunately it was in the summer, and it was quite pleasant weath-er, but the journey home that night took about two and a half to three hours so we didn't want too many of those, but fortunately we didn't get many. A typical journey continued to accelerate quite nicely and smoothly and, of course, in the '50s, you still had 'clickety click, clickety click' as the train went over the rails and the joint. Nobody ever talked about, or even thought about cracked rails, what were they? Nowadays of course they are all welded into six hundred foot lengths of track so as to reduce the number of 'clickety clicks' which were really very damaging to the wheel sets and I think do lead, to some extent, along with leaves, into fractured rails and fractured wheels as well.
John Mitchell

About 1950, we did have a railway accident across the road one evening. I think one or two things were derailed, you know, and a friend of mine was on the train and got her glasses smashed.
Mary Young

Being interested in railways, I always used to try and go up and down by steam train while they lasted and that was always quite fun. The carriages were quite reasonably swept and dusted inside and they had proper cushions, unlike the things you sit on now. There was an overhead rack for coats and briefcases and umbrellas. If you were carrying anything larger, you probably put it in the guard's van or maybe travelled with it in the rush hour. If it was a goods train going down to Basingstoke or somewhere and climbing up the hill, it could be putting out a lot of smoke. Some of the non-stop down trains could make a terrific amount of smoke.
John Davenport

There's always a deposit on the windows – even though now there's no – or very few – steam trains, there's a certain amount of deposit that comes from the rails.
Emily Gloster

Of course the trains used to get more dirty in those days with the steam, so you soon learnt to travel with your back to the engine if you could, bcause if you had the windows open the bits used to blow in. If you were facing them, you see, you got the full blast!
Joan Roberts

If you stood on the bridge and the steam train went underneath, you would come out with smuts in your eyes. You were coated with grime if you did it often enough.

You see steam trains today occasionally as specials go through Woking but all those trains are in immaculate condition. They've been lovingly polished by the preservation societies and they gleam, but the trains back in 1967 or '66 were absolutely filthy. The locomotives themselves, whatever colour they were meant to be, were always black or grey with grime and dirt and soot. British Rail knew that all these trains were going to be scrapped so they were maintained to keep them going, but not maintained to make them work better and more efficiently for the future. In particular, they were not cleaned. So locomotives that started off in nice British Railways Southern green would still be black, so they really looked disgraceful, but that's only because everyone knew they were going to be scrapped.
Guy Consterdine

Evacuees arrive at Woking station, 1939 *Woking History Society*

Necropolis Company line with Brookwood Station on the left and the gates to Brookwood Cemetery on the right, 1938
Lens of Sutton

The Necropolis Company were a lot of quite smart businessmen who decided that London had a major problem in dealing with the dead. All the churchyards were full and they managed to buy an enormous chunk of Surrey where the London bodies were going to be brought.

You can't pretend that steam trains were clean. It did tend to come in through the windows even if they were shut and the upholstery got dirty and yes, they were generally grubby. If you stood on the bridge and the steam train went underneath, you would come out with smuts in your eyes. You were coated with grime if you did it often enough.

People didn't tend to leave litter behind like they do now, because there weren't the takeaway cups and fast foods and all the wrappers and bits and pieces. They were generally much tidier. If anything, it was cigarette packets or wrappers or things like that.

The Necropolis Company were a lot of quite smart businessmen who decided that London had a major problem in dealing with the dead. All the churchyards were full and the population was growing and consequently, so was the number of people dying. They managed to buy an enormous chunk of Surrey from the Earl of Onslow and this was where the London bodies were going to be brought. They even had a special station at Waterloo and a branch line off behind Brookwood Station that ran into the cemetery, so that you ran a special train with mourners and hearses direct from Waterloo into the cemetery. A lot of Woking is on what was Necropolis land at one time.
John Davenport

When the Doodlebugs came you used to look out and see them coming and you used to hope, if they were coming in your direction, they'd pass over your train before they'd fall.

In the blackout all you had was a tiny little blue light in the middle of the carriage. The windows were partly screened, so that they didn't show a general light travelling along. If you looked out, you saw nothing because the whole region was blacked out at night – no streetlights, nothing – it was interesting. Yes, you could see the stars all right because there was no upward glare from anywhere at all.
Derek Haycroft

They had blinds for the blackout which you had to pull down and you were meant to keep them down.
John Davenport

Travelling to London, as I was, the line would get bombed quite often of a night-time and at Wimbledon, they'd stop and say, 'All off, all off, line down.' Of course, we soon realised there was no point trying to come home because there were shelters under Whitehall, so we started sleeping up there.

When the Doodlebugs came you used to look out and see them coming and you used to hope, if they were coming in your direction, they'd pass over your train before they'd fall.
Serena Whiteman

In the blackout all you had was a tiny little blue light in the middle of the carriage. The windows were partly screened, so that they didn't show a general light travelling along.

There were favourite spots around Woking. There were parts along the Broadway in Woking we would go and of course it was not long after the nationalisation of the railways with the variety of engines and trains that you got. And of course Woking was, and still is, a railway centre, but it was a bit more so in those days because there were troop movements. I can remember a troop train coming into Woking, which was hauled by a most peculiar engine from some distant part of the country. The carriages were different. It had obviously come from the Midlands or from the North and all these troops were hanging out of the windows, shouting and screaming. I don't know why it stayed in Woking, whether it got loaded up, or discharged troops at Woking I don't know, but Pirbright Camp was quite active in those days and it still is of course to some extent.
Richard Barnard

The trains these days are a nightmare, with delays and cancellations. I don't remember the railways being such nonsense – you got on a train and you got there on the dot. It's odd really, there's just no improvement of any kind – I don't see any.
Wendy Davenport

The only time we had anything at Woking was when it celebrated one hundred and fifty years of the railway in Woking which was 1988, and that was the only time it got dressed up. They had a collection of engines parked in the goods yard that had worked through Woking over the years, that you could crawl over and they ran the odd special train. It was quite fun.
John Davenport

Steam and diesel locomotives at Woking 150 Exhibition, 1988
Graham Cartland Glover

Woking Railway Station, goods yard and town centre, 1983
Graham Cartland Glover

The horse knew the round and the horse would keep walking and stop at particular places along the road and all the milkman had to do was get out and run with the pints and just say, 'Gee!'

You'd still get your divi on a funeral. From cradle to grave almost, they supplied your needs.

When we went to a private company, not a big company like Sainsbury's, you sat down. It was really an absolutely social occasion.

5. Shops and Shopping

The bleach man used to come and my mum used to buy bleach and, after so many bottles, she got a free tea towel.

The first Sainsbury's in Woking was in Chertsey Road. This shows the traditional Christmas poultry display, 1920 *The Sainsbury Archive*

Sainsbury's, it obviously wasn't like the Sainsbury's of today. Oh no, and of course I used to love going into Sainsbury's because they always used to beat the butter, and that was lovely to see them, you know, beat all the butter. When I say beating, I mean patting it, great big blocks, and then they used to get their cutters and take a piece off and then pat it into shape, and put it on the scales, you know and wrap it up. And the cheese was done the same. Great big cheeses, you'd have the fascination of seeing them cut it with the wires you know, and everything. And they used to do lovely corner pieces, so only on one end you'd just get a square of rind and all the rest was just cheese, you know. And of course all matured beautifully, you know, lovely, to see the cheese being cut and that. And the bacon was always, you know, you picked your piece and you told them what thickness you wanted, and they'd do your rashers on the bacon machine. All that kind of thing. It was fascinating to watch, you know.
Peggy Goring

Mr Wearing the chemist, very often people would go to him rather than have to pay to go to the doctors; they would pay to go to him, they would go and he was very good at advising what he thought was suitable.
Ada Green

Great big cheeses, you'd have the fascination of seeing them cut it with the wires. They used to do lovely corner pieces, so only on one end you'd just get a square of rind and all the rest was just cheese.

Gloster's, early 20th century *The Lightbox*

In Woking we were just called a village when I came here. It wasn't, but everybody called it, 'Going down to the village.' Well, it was a very limited shopping centre. I don't think it was ever written up as a village, but we called it that because that's about all there was. Just a few shops.
Katharine Buchanan

I always remember the butchers because they used to have rabbits hanging all the way round there and they used to hang these rabbits up by the back leg and have a little tin under the head to catch the blood, I suppose, and I was always fascinated by these rows of rabbits hanging up outside his butcher's shop.
Bert Hollis

There was a lovely chemist in the town, which was called Wearing's. It was run by the father and daughter. Lovely shop. And I must admit I was only saying the other day, 'Do you remember if ever you had a cough you used to go and see Mr Wearing, and he used to make up his own mixture?' He wouldn't be allowed to do it now, of course, but I tell you what - and so much advice and that, you know? I think it worked, there was something in it, and it wasn't all that unpleasant from what I can remember. Always used to go there for it, always.
Peggy Goring

Old Woking High Street, 1900 *The Lightbox*

You always stayed with the same surgery. I think that was something my mother taught us, you know, you stayed, you didn't pop from pillar – like with shopping, we always got our meat at Akehurst's and they knew you and you could get a round of beef for 2/6d. Yes, well that was a family business and his wife used to sit at the desk and she always called him Sir and the meat was considered very good there and of course it all hung up outside, great big carcasses, and at Christmas there would be the geese and the turkeys all hung up with their feathers on and nobody bothered. You bought your turkey, brought it home, sometimes people would pluck them themselves or otherwise you would get the butcher to pluck it, and then further up the road there was the shoe shop which had reasonably priced shoes.

On the corner of Church Street was a tobacconist and he had a machine that he made cigarettes and you could watch him. He would make a great big long pencil-shaped thing and he had this particular knife, would cut them into lengths, and tobacco and matches, because my father always smoked a pipe and he always had to have shag. There was a delicatessen down there where Mr Lush sold ham, and next door there was this paper shop and tobacconist, and my father used to like Lloyds newspaper and one day one of my cousins was staying with us, apparently, and she went down to see Father, and Father said, 'Now will you go up to the shop and get me some saveloys,' which Mr Lush sold, and she tripped off up the road; when she got there, she went in the paper shop and asked for seven Lloyds. Fortunately my father kept an eye on her to see where she was going and of course he had to pop up quickly and tell the man he didn't want seven Lloyds, it was next door for saveloys because they were very good, because they could be recommended, you never queried about getting poisoned.
Ada Green

There was nothing particularly great in the shopping line. There was a branch of Sainsbury's with old fashioned counters and all that kind of thing, but there was very, very little shopping in the town. There was a butcher's and greengrocer's and baker's but nothing very exciting. It's gone from that to what we've got now, with the odd hiccup in between, and quite a lot of what happened in between was definitely not an improvement, but now I think it's generally better.
John Davenport

We lived in Lambourne Crescent. Yeah, but we were very lucky. We had marvellous neighbours. There was always somebody who went shopping so you automatically went along and said, you know – 'What did you need?' So we would take it in turns, almost, to do the shopping. And I can remember my children being ill once and a neighbour's father was there and he walked all the way to West Byfleet and got the prescription for me. The people in Woking weren't terribly friendly. No, Woking and West Byfleet, no. A friend of mine went to buy something on hire purchase and, because you come from Sheerwater, they said, 'No.' You know it was very... The orphanage children used to come to school here and so you had, sort of, groups, but the children always said they came from Woking instead of Sheerwater.
Betty Heller

The only thing you hear Woking people moaning about is the parking, isn't it? I can't really understand Woking Council in a way. They want you to go shopping in Woking but they don't want you to park, you know. I know I've heard one or two people moan about where can we park. Cars rule our lives, really, in a way they didn't when we were younger. We had the four-legged cart didn't we? So that's the only thing I think they ought to think about and I mean they're trying to keep us away from the Victoria at night now by charging, aren't they? But there you are, but never mind. Progress! But all the old shops have gone aren't they, that's, you know, which we did rely on that we could get something now, plus you got to have everything that's wrapped up haven't you, now? If you go and buy a few screws it's wrapped up, it's only ten. Ten, yes, you want six and you can only get five, can't you and all that caper, you know.
John W. Francis

I always used to buy my mum and dad sweets on the way home. At Sheerwater, because in them days you didn't open your wage packet. You took it home. So, I used to get paid, I think, weekly on a Thursday, take it home and I always bought my sweets on Friday. I used to go to the pictures once a week, which was 3 shillings. And just clothes and in them days you had Provident cheques. You might not know. Provident cheques were where you borrowed the money. A bit like HP, I suppose. And if you wanted a Provident cheque for £5, a man would come round. Then you pay it back weekly. And there was certain shops that would take them. Not every shop would take them so you had to find out which shop would take a Provident cheque. For clothes and things like that. It was like

a form of HP. You didn't have to go to a special bank or anything. No, the man used to actually call at the door. I mean, my mum and dad had had them for years and he used to come to the door and then, if you wanted to borrow say £20, they'd give you like – like gift vouchers really. Then you'd take them to the shop and then every week he'd come to collect the money like they used to collect the rent at the door in them days.
Janet Hicks

Meals were a very strict affair. We all had to sit down at the table and always have our meal together.

Meals were a very strict affair. We all had to sit down at the table, you know, and always have our meal together. And I remember Sunday lunch was usually – what was the cut of beef grandma used to get? – she used to get a huge chunk of beef, that was our Sunday dinner. We used to have that roast on Sunday, we'd have it cold on Monday, hashed up or stewed or something on Tuesday and it usually lasted till Wednesday. She always used to get this large chunk of beef from the butcher in Goldsworth Road.
Bert Hollis

Yes, we had to get the shopping and if we hadn't got it right, we went back and you could bike from Woodham to Woking, park your bike outside the shop, go in and get whatever it was and come out again and the bike was still there. Wherever you left your bike, it was still there.
Wendy Davenport

You could buy a lot for a penny. Not the pence now, but the old penny, half-penny, penny. Kids used to be in there, 'cause if you got a penny pocket money a week you were lucky. So when you think now that tuppence ha'penny is sixpence isn't it, so it wasn't even one of your half p's you get now, but that was what you had for the week. Ooh, um, oh what else could you buy? Fruit, if fruit was there, you'd buy a big apple or couple of big apples, you went in sweet shops, you could get a big bag of sweets, toffees, anything, oh all sorts of things, yeah, it went a long way that did.

And another thing, you don't have Pie and Eel shops now do you? They were lovely.
Irene Oldall

Coins from before decimalisation
Martin Bowman

Milk deliveries from Durnford Farm Dairy, Woodham, 1920s *Lyndon Davies*

We had the dairy on the corner of Monument Road where we used to take the milk jug for a pint or a quart. You took your milk jug up there and they ladled it out of the milk churn into – either you wanted a pint or a quart because you had the three size milk jugs in those days, half pint, pint and quart. You had to carry it very carefully. And then the bakery was opposite where we got the bread when it was still hot from the oven and ate the corner of the crust before we got it home. I remember it was ninepence a loaf and fourpence ha'penny for a small loaf. And the hot cross buns! – I mean hot cross bun day, you didn't have them all the year; they were cooked on the Good Friday and they brought them round to your house. You either went up and got them or the girl used to come round with her big basket to the door with the bread. She brought bread round as well and hot cross buns all hot and I was the eldest of the three youngest children, so I was allowed – I used to look forward to Good Friday because I was allowed to take my dad and auntie up a hot cross bun and a cup of tea in bed. That was my yearly event, take them up a hot cross bun.
Betty Curtis

You took your milk jug up there and they ladled it out of the milk churn into – either you wanted a pint or a quart because you had the three size milk jugs in those days, half pint, pint and quart.

Up Monument Road towards the Lion Works, going into Princess Road, there used to be an absolutely gorgeous baker's on the corner, with all fresh bread. They baked on the premises. The bakehouse was just behind. You could smell the smell of bread for miles, you know? It was lovely. And there was old Mrs Farris, on the corner of Frailey Hill there. Shops, there was loads of little shops. It's a shame that they've all disappeared. But I hear tell that the corner shop's coming back again. They were saying that all these little shops that have disappeared they're starting to come back again so let's hope they do.

It was a lovely old town, it really was. You know where McDonald's is now? That was the main street and you'd have walls at the bottom and you'd have the shops either side, going down there. And you'd have a wet fish shop, going down towards where Wearing's the chemist was. You'd have Boots the chemist. You'd have Freeman, Hardy and Willis, Skinner's, the shoe shop, and, on the other side, there'd be the Maypole – oh, I remember the Maypole! They used to have – it was like a big drum by the door and my Mum used to put my pushchair there when I was little. It was used to soak dried peas. And I used to keep putting my hand in and pinching them, you know? These dried peas. They knocked that down to build Asda. But it was Fine Fare first, before it was Asda. Then Asda took it over. The day Fine Fare opened you went in there and they were going round giving everybody free gifts. Fine Fare was a lovely shop. That was the first supermarket in Woking. That was in the '60s or '70s. And then Asda took it over and they were quite good. And it was a shame because they closed down. I think they had really great problems with the roof leaking so they sold it. They said it would cost over a million to repair the roof but, if they done what the people that bought it did, which was put another floor on with a dome on the top – cured the problem. And we lost our store, which was the only big supermarket.

All we've got in the town now is Sainsbury's. And that's only quite a small store really. It's handy for the old people. Now they've built the new Safeway, it's not so bad. But if you wanted to do a really big shop you'd have to go out of the town. I mean, when I was a kid if you wanted anything decent you used to have to go on the bus, go to Guildford. Because Guildford was always a better town than Woking.

They used to have – it was like a big drum by the door and my Mum used to put my pushchair there when I was little. It was used to soak dried peas. And I used to keep putting my hand in and pinching them, you know?

Working in the Co-op was quite an experience, working down there. We had a manager. He was a really nice chap. Mr Herbert. We used to have all our regular customers in there, you know? Before we went decimal. We used to have all the old people that came in that used to have their dividend numbers. We'd have to put their numbers up on the machine when we took the money at the till. Then we put their numbers on the machine. You'd have like a machine you'd push up to one, then another one up to two. Say your number was – I can still remember mine – 7681. Seven, up to seven, then to eight, down to six, one. And then when you rang the money up it was recorded on your dividend. And, I always remember an old

Fine Fare, 1965. The site is now occupied by the Big Apple and, behind it, the H.G Wells Centre *Woking History Society*

lady called Mrs Fisher, because she came in to me and she said, 'What do you think about this referendum, Pam? About us going into the Common Market?' So I said to her, 'I'll tell you what, Mrs Fisher' – I was putting out – I'd just put out the sugar on the side and I was just stocking the freezer with butter, you know, the fridge with butter and that (butter was two shillings and ten pence a pound – that's for two blocks – and sugar was one and sixpence for a two pound packet) and I said to Mrs Fisher, 'You see that sugar there?
I'm willing to bet a week's wages that within three years that over doubles. And this butter will over treble.' And she said, 'Don't be stupid. They won't do things like that.' What was it in three years time? The butter was nearly what was 10 shillings, 50p, 60p for two blocks and the sugar had gone up to about 38p to 40p.

We were general assistants. We'd go out and cut the bacon on the bacon ma-chine if they wanted their bacon. Cut the ham, which we cooked, incidentally, on the premises. It was beautiful ham as well. It was very different to a modern supermar-ket. Oh yeah. Much different. I mean, we'd have the sides of bacon come in and we'd have to bone it all out before we could cut it, you know. It was a sort of self-serve. Yes, we'd have the baskets by the door and people would go round and pick up what they wanted, come to the till. We had two tills, which was quite a lot. We used to have quite a good turnover there because we had so many people that belonged to the Co-op. It was an institution, you know? It really was. This is how the divi worked. You'd get money. You would get like a cheque. And if it was enough you could buy a week's groceries or more. You know, with your dividend.

They even did it on funerals. You'd still get your divi on a funeral. I always remem-ber Mrs Tapp, when her father died. She came in and she'd had her father's funeral through the Co-op and she said, 'Oh, I've come in to pay my father's funeral bill. Can you record it for my dividend, please?' I'll always remember that. Oh, yes, funerals were all part of the Co-op. From cradle to grave almost, they supplied your needs.

And shoppers were members. You were actually members and you got a vote. Our local head office was Addlestone, the old Addlestone, as it was. We used to go over there. I used to go over there on a Saturday afternoon, do a bit of shopping and they'd have a fashion parade up in the ladies' department and we'd get a cup of tea and a biscuit, watching the models modelling the fashions up in the Co-op.

We didn't suffer from Green Shield Stamps when they came in. I think we collected them but we still bought our groceries because you didn't buy groceries with Green Shield Stamps. That was just goods. But no, the Co-op never suffered like that. I think what made them have to scale down their operations was the fact that all the other big supermarkets – Sainsbury's was getting bigger, Tesco's came in – because when Tesco's first started it was a little shop with a pull-down blind.

I remember one day in the Co-op. There was old Mrs Martin, she worked there for years and years and years. She's got very, very frail. She now lives in a house down by The Wheatsheaf. But she was a crafty lady because when we used to have anybody from Head Office come, she was one of these ladies that always looked busy but wasn't. She'd go along facing up the tins, you know? Because they have to be all put in, in a certain way. You can't just shove tins in any way. You have to have the label facing outwards and everything and she'd go along and there'd

be us chatting when the bosses walked in and she'd be facing up all the tins. Yes, she was a nice old stick though. We got on very, very well. We were like a family, a happy family down there. It was a shame that that ever went. It's now, as you know, a decorator's shop, Akehurst's.
Pamela Peachey

They even did it on funerals. You'd still get your divi on a funeral. From cradle to grave almost, they supplied your needs.

The shops are totally different now. We used to have a shoe shop, a toy shop, an off-licence, a Co-op, two sweet shops. One called Deakin's, one called Duff's, two local people. Two grocer's, one butcher's. Dry cleaner's, I think that's been there for a long time. A café and a shop we used to call the oil shop because when I was young you didn't have centrally heating, you had either a coal fire or paraffin burning fires. And everyone referred to it as the oil shop because it was the only place to get the oil for the fires. So it was always called the oil shop but it was a hardware store.

We had five wet fish shops: the Mac Fisheries had two (they had one in Guildford Road and one in Chertsey Road); and there was Stubb's, the fishmonger's down Chobham Road; Seaman's had two shops one was in the Goldsworth Road, I don't know where the other one was[2]. And there were three or four butchers' shops.
Barry Pope

2. It was at 87 Walton Road. (Ed.)

In Woodham, the milkman came with a horse and cart – a beautiful horse.
We used to follow him all the way round and they were actually more economic than the vans now. The horse knew the round and the horse would keep walking and stop at particular places along the road and all the milkman had to do was get out and run with the pints and just say, 'Gee!' and he'd move along to the next stop you see, so the milkman wasn't forever in and out of the van stopping and starting. He was on the trot the whole time going round and the horse just knew exactly what to do. The vegetables came round with the horse and cart as well. They did a round of the Woodham Estate and they came from Sharman's in Maybury and he was the local greengrocer and he came round, so you got that to the house as well. You see the mothers couldn't drive, the mothers had no cars.
Wendy Davenport

Benham's from Chobham was a bigger place, that had a mill and that down there, they used to come, bring groceries, you ordered it for one week.
They'd come Saturday afternoon, mother would give them the order for the next week. You had to order it a week in advance.

Well, the butcher was in Knaphill – Grimlins and Webb. They used to come round with the horse and cart Monday, Tuesday, in fact they used to come round every day and you would have paid eight pence for a pound of stewing beef. And he used to come round and bring what you ordered one day, and then take the order for the next day.

At the weekends you had like a shoulder of lamb or a bit of beef; that lasted Sunday and Monday mostly. Then we had a coal strike. The coalman was from

Knaphill. He never came for six weeks, and mother had a good heap of coal, and she burned wood and that with it, and Mrs Butler two doors away, she ran out of coal and that, so if she made a pie, apple pie or anything, she used to bring it up and Mum used to cook it for her.

The baker used to come from Knaphill, Queen's Road Knaphill, and a woman used to come and she had two great big baskets about that size – round – one each side of her handlebars, and she rode from Knaphill to West End with it. And one on the back of her bicycle. And she used to come more or less every day. I don't think she'd come Wednesdays. I think she come every day delivering bread. Yes, she

Horse-drawn cart delivering milk in the floods in Old Woking, 1928 *The Lightbox*

used to come and she used to ride this bicycle from Knaphill with these two great big baskets and one on the back. And she never complained, rain, blow or snow. And she had like a piece of mackintosh that went over the baskets if it was raining. Wouldn't be hygienic nowadays though would it! No.
Elsie Goff

The horse knew the round and the horse would keep walking and stop at particular places along the road and all the milkman had to do was get out and run with the pints and just say, 'Gee!'

We used to have a 'Penny Man', who used to come round in a caravan. It was a little shop in it. It was wonderful. Fish man used to come round on Fridays in a thing as well. That was that wet fish. Yes. Fresh fish every Friday. The charabanc that came round had everything. I mean, you used to go in a little door there and he'd be behind the little counter there and he had everything. It was like a little groceries on wheels. I'll always remember that. Used to ding his bell and out you'd go there. All sorts of other trades people came round.

We used to have a vegetable man as well. He used to do all the vegetables, potatoes and all that. And the bleach man – I mean, we used to have a lot of deliveries in them days. The bleach man used to come and my mum used to buy bleach and, after so many bottles, she got a free tea towel. I'll always remember that. Yes. He was, literally, just called 'the bleach man.' That was all he sold. But the Penny Man was wonderful. Used to go and buy like four chews for a penny. That's what you called him. I don't know why he was called the Penny Man. Probably, because you could buy something for a penny off him but that's how he was called the Penny Man. But the fish man was lovely because my mum always used to buy fresh fish and we always had fish on Fridays. She did it herself, in batter, and it was lovely.
Janet Hicks

The bleach man used to come and my mum used to buy bleach and, after so many bottles, she got a free tea towel.

The butcher used to call twice a week, the grocer used to call once a week. You'd have a vegetable man who called, a milkman and a baker. Everyone sort of called.
Betty Heller

A man used to come round with a big caravan and we called him the Penny Man. He used to sell sweets for the children and then he started getting groceries, everything he sold, he came round every day and we used to buy bread and sugar. That was a real lifeline for us. He was a German man. He was lovely. He came with his knife and fork, he told us all his story and he did very well. And all the kids knew the Penny Man, he was the Penny Man and I think a lot of people used to be able to buy their stuff when he came at the end of the week.
Ida Jenkin

A butcher came round in his van so you could get your meat. There was another one came round, big van, which had – oh, the milkman, the Co-op milkman – he came round and delivered; then there was a great big – more of a lorry – and that came round with all your fruit and veg on, you could go out and buy it. Another one, Mac Fisheries, came round with wet fish and that and the one the kids all liked was the Penny Man. He was a big van and he got all the sweets and bits in, he was always called the Penny Man, 'cause then, you could buy a lot for a penny.
Irene Oldall

When we went to a private company, not a big company like Sainsbury's, you sat down. It was really an absolutely social occasion.

T H Bungey, bakers and confectioners, Church Path, ready for deliveries, 1916
Mrs Christine Heater

When we went to a private company, not a big company like Sainsbury's, you sat down. When you came in, you sat down and he said, 'Morning Madam, and how are you today and what would you like?' And then he would go and get your margarine and give you a discussion about it and get your sugar, and it was really an absolutely social occasion. But the nice thing about it was, even the International, a big shop like that, they delivered your goods, you didn't carry them home and that was really very nice. When you think that now,

as an old lady, I have to bring it home. Any rate, it wasn't so in those days. All these young men, young boys on bicycles with big baskets in the front with the goods coming along, and they'd say, 'It'll be there soon after you're home,' and they timed it so well, that it never seemed to arrive before you did.
Serena Whiteman

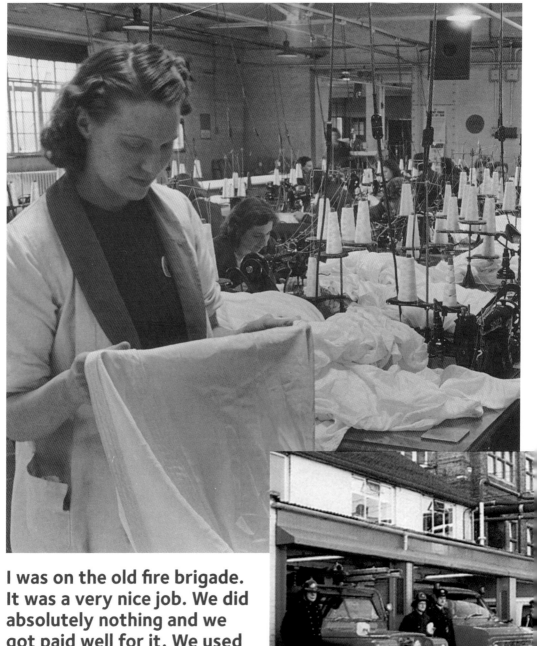

I was on the old fire brigade. It was a very nice job. We did absolutely nothing and we got paid well for it. We used to start at seven. We used to sit around all day, watching telly, hoping that the bells would go down for a fire but we didn't get very many.

They'd have 'Music While You Work' on and that was lovely, you know, you was all singing away there while we were working.

In those days you only had Christmas Day and Boxing Day off.

6. Working in Woking

When I first went to work there in 1954, there were about two thousand people there and when I left there were a hundred.

I went to work for Ebison's in Maybury Road, which was a little father and son garage and I started an apprenticeship there then, when I was fourteen, and course I drove my first vehicle there.
It was a Ford Model 'T' that belonged to an ironmonger down the High Street in Woking – right down the far end on the left there was an ironmonger called Harkers. He had two of these Ford Model 'T's and they had a big square boxy body on the back and he had tanks of paraffin in the back and on a piece of string hanging down the back he had all the measuring cans, that used to rattle as he went along – solid tyres these things had on them. And he used to go round selling paraffin at houses and I drove one of those and, of course, it's vastly different from the cars, they didn't have a gear lever, you just pushed pedals in and out to make them go. And one of the mechanics, or the chap who I was working with – I was his boy – he allowed me to drive one of these things down Portugal Road in Woking and he was running alongside me, 'cause they didn't even have doors on them, they just had open bits where the doors were. And he was running along the side, he says, 'Now let your left foot half way up,' and the thing would go chugging along and then he'd say, 'Now let your foot all the way up,' and I drove that down Portugal Road into the garage at the bottom where they had a ramp to put them up and down to inspect the underneath of them. And I worked there till I was sixteen, then I left there when I was sixteen and went to work for Morris House in Commercial Road.
Bert Hollis

I didn't think much of the job because I used to go home smothered in ink because I used to clean the machines down, so after a week I gave my notice in.

I left when I got to fourteen and I just left and I didn't get a job, so after a couple of days Mr Bliaux said, 'Have you got a job?' I said, 'No' – or my mother or father said no – and he said, 'Right, I know Mr Silk and I know Mr Bridger and one or two other builders, I'll have a word with them, see if I can get you in, because evidently you did fairly well at woodwork classes,' and eventually, he got me a job with Silks and we were definitely the best builders in the area. We built the best houses, all up through Worplesdon and the Hockering and he wouldn't take on anything he didn't think was good enough. I was an apprentice carpenter and joiner. I was sent out with a lorry driver to help load bags of cement up at Woking Station. If it wasn't the first day, it was close and I came home and told my father and he wasn't very pleased. He said, 'I thought you went there to be a carpenter,' so I think he had a word with Mr Silk. He said, 'That boy's got to do as he's told.'
Bill Curtis

You could have three lights put in your house, you didn't pay, but you paid when you put a shilling in the meter.

There was somebody by the name of Dallen, he was a jointer at Woking Electric. I got talking to him and he says, 'Why don't you come to the Electric if you're interested in that way?' So I went for an interview with Mr Woods who was the Manager at Woking Electric. 'Can you write? Are you strong?' and that was about the interview and he said, 'Well, I can't offer you a place because we're full up at the moment.' We didn't go as apprentices, we went as electricians' mates. So I went for an interview with Woking News and Mail. The manager's name was Fraser. I started on the Monday and I didn't think much of the job because I used to go home smothered in ink because I used to clean the machines down, so after a week I gave my notice in. I lasted a week and had to do another week and he said that he would never employ me again under no circumstances. So I left there on the Friday and I started Woking Electric on the Monday. You had to go in the entrance in North Road and report to a foreman by the name of Mr Veal and from then on we just went helping electricians until we learnt the trade.

We were doing domestic installations, you know. We used to do a scheme called 'the three lights.' You could have three lights put in your house, you didn't pay, but you paid when you put a shilling in the meter. You only got ten pennyworth of electricity, the other tuppence went to pay for the installation, so we done quite a few of those. Some people would only get the hall light and the kitchen and the lounge, or the sitting room as it was. You wouldn't get any upstairs because that would mean a bit extra work and I think you only had a day and a half to do it, which seems a long time now but it was quite an effort sometimes to do that.

I think now we should have set more houses alight because we only worked by candles.

People were still using candles upstairs and I think now we should have set more houses alight because we only worked by candles. In the roof, you know, you'd have a candle, candle flat on the joist, stick it down and hope you didn't knock it over, so, you know, we didn't have any torches in those days.
John W Francis

A Model 'T' of Ebison's, Ford dealers, dressed for the 'Wokympia' trade fair, 1929
Lyndon Davies

FORD SERVICE DEPOT

EBISON'S OF **WOKING**

6 CHOBHAM RD

094 PC

My apprenticeship! Well, it was a four year apprenticeship. Most apprenticeships were five years. It was a four year apprenticeship, day release at Guildford College. And so you'd spend one day a week at Guildford College, running all the background and the paperwork, and the rest of the week you'd work in the factory.

The first year you'd make your own toolbox and make all your own tools to go in the toolbox. And then from the second year onwards you'd work on the shop floor but you'd only be given very simple jobs to do until, you know, you got a little bit more into the apprenticeship and, towards the end, you'd be doing the same as a normal man would be doing on the machine next to you. So you were doing the same job. And at that time they started introducing computer machines. Now my factory where I worked there were twenty lathes, which actually turn metal. There were about the same number of mills, they were grinding machines, and there was something called a spark eroder machine, which used to have a point on it and pass an electric current through the point and actually burn the metal into a shape. Well at that time, when I'd just started my apprenticeship, computer machines started arriving to do all this and take the men away from the shop floor. But they ran on long strips of tape and it would take a man a day, day and a half, to punch out all the punch holes in a long reel of tape before it could go into the machine but once it was in, the machine would just keep operating all the time and all you had to do was sharpen the tools and load the material. And that's all you did. So, it was the change coming into the computerised age.
Barry Pope

The first year you'd make your own toolbox and make all your own tools to go in the toolbox. From the second year you'd work on the shop floor but you'd only be given very simple jobs until you got more into the apprenticeship.

I looked in the Woking News and Mail and it said, 'Electrical Apprentice required' and I went down there myself and I got the job and it was an apprenticeship with Unwins. They are printers – still there today[3] – but where you used to get the compositors and the monotype people, the keyboard operators, over the years it just diminished to – probably you had about a hundred and fifty people – it went down to about ten people and they're still cutting down on staff today. One of my recollections of the compositors: all the old compositors used to have what they call snuff. They used to pinch it and put it at their nose and sniff it and that used to give them a clear head for the rest of the day, or it was supposed to have done.

And I always remember when I first started it was twenty five shillings a week and when I signed apprenticeship forms, it went down to nineteen and sixpence which wasn't very much money. However, it went up about five shillings each year and in the finish it was a seven year apprenticeship, which I honestly thought was cheap labour, but they cut two years off, or the government did, so you only had to do a five year apprenticeship. I started there in '46 and I completed, I

3. Unwins have now ceased production in Woking. (Ed.)

think, one of the last people to do fifty years service to a company.

This didn't happen when I was apprenticed but if a person got out of his apprenticeship they used to put ink all over him and all sorts of things and oil and you name it, and he usually finished up in the river which is underneath Unwins, and they did that as a sort of ceremony in the latter days, in the '70s, really, but when I came out of my apprenticeship, they didn't do it, thank goodness, but there we go.

I used to work with a gentleman called Mr Parnell who loved doing pranks and I always remember Mr Parnell – and the Managing Director there was Mr Edmunds – and we stood outside his office and he had a trumpet and blew the Last Post, only for him to put the trumpet between the papers. We made off at haste, only to be followed by Mr Edmunds to say, 'Mr Parnell, did you hear anything there?' So he said, 'No.' And Mr Edmunds said, 'I thought I heard a trumpet blow with the Last Post.' Mr Parnell's reply was 'Well, you know what they say, if you hear the Last Post, they're coming for you, so I should be very careful.'

Unwins had allotments, they used to have their sports day out there and the Unwins used to turn up with their trilby on and that, gloves on, because she didn't like people shaking hands with her unless she had her gloves on. This was Mrs Unwin.

But, with Unwins, how I got on, I was an electrician and there was a lot of building going on and I sort of did everything there, put all the lights in, all sorts of things, and then it went from there – 'Oh he can look after that,' or, 'Who can do First Aid? Oh he can look after that' and in the finish I built up quite an empire doing all these jobs but, you know, it was interesting.

There used to be about thirty people in what they called 'the Services', or the engineers, and you used to have the roads to do, the sports fields and everything. And over the years, even with that, the sports field used to have one man there every day of the week out there, cutting it, doing it. And in the finish the Unwin brothers said, 'Well, what're we doing, we can't afford to do that,' so that was knocked on the head.

Unwins had allotments, they had all sorts of things. They used to have their sports day out there and the Unwins used to turn up with their trilby on and that, gloves on, because she didn't like people shaking hands with her unless she had her gloves on. This was Mrs Unwin. And everybody used do the running and bicycle race and you name it. This was held on Unwins sports field.
Philip Ledger

Unwins Printers by the River Wey at Old Woking *The Lightbox*

Monotype keyboards at Unwins, 1940s *Unwins*

Well, if you wanted to work in a shop, you'd have to go into Woking because there wasn't a lot of shops in Sheerwater, there were shops but you know, West Byfleet, I mean, it wasn't looking like it is now because West Byfleet didn't have Waitrose, didn't have Woolworths. You had a very good shop there, I think it was Garnett Jones – well you'd have to be a certain type of person to have got a job in there! – you know, so I wouldn't even have thought of going, you know, applying to go there to work. You could go in the laundry, there was Ashley Cook's, there was the Alpine Laundry in Arnold Road and you could go – as I did – I went to work at the Orphanage, the Railway Orphanage. I suppose you could have been a domestic in the hospital, you know, because we had the other hospital in Woking then.
Elsie Stranks

My home was the Alpine Laundry in Eve Road. It had been a hand laundry when my father took it over. We moved there about 1932-33 when I was about eighteen months old and my earliest memories of the laundry really is of a very large area with lots and lots of lines going across where all the sheets were hung, and the smell of sort of steam and Lux soap, because that's what they used in those days, soap flakes – we didn't have the detergent as we have now. There were large washing machines, very large ones with big sort of doors on them and everything was pushed into the washing machines. Most of the clients were people who lived in the large homes around Woking and father would collect the washing on a Monday and would then deliver it on a Friday. Most people didn't like their articles to be named so my father had to devise some way of naming the article so we could retrieve them after they had all been washed, which, of course as you can imagine, caused some problems with mix-ups of sending the wrong shirt to the wrong house.

In those days, of course, a lot of people still had maids in their homes and, of course, they had uniforms, so one of the main items of equipment was the goffering irons which were almost like little tongs for doing your hair, very similar to that. We had one lady, Mrs Gardner, who was a whizz at doing the goffering for the maids' cuffs and their little head dresses that they wore. That didn't last very long, the goffering. I think the maids were sort of – by the time the War came – they didn't have maids in the big houses like they did in the early '30s.

My earliest memories of the laundry really is of a very large area with lots and lots of lines going across where all the sheets were hung, and the smell of sort of steam and Lux soap flakes.

Things were hung on lines to dry and then they were ironed. We had long long tables I remember with these gas irons and they would thump down on the tables. When I saw that film, Dr Zhivago, in there there's a scene where she's ironing and banging the iron onto the ironing board; it really brought back memories of my childhood and I remembered these irons being slapped down on the sort of padded tables as they ironed the sheets and the shirts.

When I saw that film, Dr Zhivago, there's a scene where she's ironing and banging the iron onto the ironing board; it brought back memories of my childhood and these irons being slapped down on the padded tables as they ironed the sheets and the shirts.

My father was an engineer so he was very clever at sort of building machines and he was always changing the laundry round and putting in new machines and adapting them. We had a very large calender and I remember the day, I must have been about seven I suppose, when the calender was delivered and really it was just a series of very large drums and you fed in the sheets in one end and they went through the rollers and came out the other end and then you folded them as they came off the machine. You had to be jolly quick at it, of course.

Two women would feed them in and two women would take them off and fold them one way and pass them on to two other ladies. It was highly intensified with labour – it needed a lot of girls really to operate these machines. All the sheets were put in great bins and then there were two girls who would shake out the sheet and hand it to the two girls who were going to feed it into the calender, then it came off the other end, then was folded by the girls and put on the tables for collection to be divided up and packed into the boxes and into the hampers. As I say, it needed a lot, a lot of labour to run the laundry, and it was 8 till 6 of course, an 8 till 6 day.

Barbara Chasemore

Working the boilers at the Rose Cottage Laundry, 1932 *Lyndon Davies*

Women sewing at GQ Parachutes, Maybury *Daily Mirror*

Well, I started at the parachute factory in September 1938, the year before the War began. I was a dressmaker, I was apprenticed. And when the crisis came – you know, that crisis in 1938 – the old dear, she gave us all the push and we all went down, and that's where I started as well.

Mr Gregory was the brains and Mr Quilter had the money. Well, they were both clever men but Gregory started off in Guildford and the first 'chute was made in his wife's sitting room, on her own machine.

There was always laughter and of course, we weren't supposed to talk very much but the rot set in and they couldn't stop us. We used to gas all day to each other.

I was on zigzagging. All the cords and bottoms, that was zigzagged into place, and after that I was on repairs for both the packs. They used to come back damaged and we would have to put them back, the same as the drawing. Imagine a pack or a 'chute that's been thrown out the back of a plane to bring it in, it's all dirty and wet and all that, and it's shrunk, and you got to put it back to the same measurements as the actual drawing. It's a bit of a job but you do it in the end. We enjoyed going to work, even in those dreadful times. There was always laughter and of course, we weren't supposed to talk very much but the rot set in and they couldn't stop us. We used to gas all day to each other. You'd get a sort of a look from your chargehand but you got on with your work just the same. It was excellent, it was an excellent factory, it was clean, it was kept clean. There was nothing wrong with it.

It was piecework. Well, you learnt to be quick you see, you learnt to be quick otherwise you didn't get any money. Bit lazy sometimes. I remember when we were on night work, if you'd finished what the Inspection had passed through for you to do, you'd just go to bed – well, not go to bed, we used to get into the bins, huge bins, with the packs in, the 'chutes already in and you fell asleep, you see, because that was shift work all through the War.
Eileen Bunyon

Well there were quite a few girls in the Inspection Room and, to inspect the 'chutes, they had like a little wooden box with a glass panel on the front with an electric light bulb inside which each of the seams had to be inspected. This 'chute, or panels, were laid over the glass and they inspected the hems, and whatever, you know, had been machined. They were looking for bad stitching and where the silk hadn't gone in the folder on the machines, right? Looking for anything, really.
Doris Francis

Well, I was there until the end of the War and then, course, made redundant 'cause married ladies went first, they were the first people to get put off so that's when I finished.

I was getting fourpence an hour at the Para and I had to go to the Lion Works and it was threepence half-penny. Later on it was piece work, so you got for how hard you'd worked and that was it.

Oh, we had a lot of fun, yeah, we had a lot of fun and it was always better paid. Of course, you always compared to the Lion Works because the Lion Works, they used to make packing things for engines, packing. And so when the first contract ended in the early days, you see, they had to put us off. Anyway, eventually I got a letter saying we have now secured another contract, so that's when I went back. I don't know quite how long, I think it was only about three months and then I went to the Lion Works you see.

At that time I was getting fourpence an hour at the Para and I had to go to the Lion Works and it was threepence half-penny. Later on it was piece work, so you got for how hard you'd worked and that was it. My father was a bricklayer and I was earning as much as he was, see.

Well, I was there until the end of the War and then, course, made redundant 'cause married ladies went first, they were the first people to get put off so that's when I finished.
Eileen Higgens

Sir Lindsey Parkinson's was the contractor, he was building it: he was building the roads, he was building the whole Sheerwater estate, he was building the drains, the roads, the houses, then he went on to the shops. They were built later. Most of the houses were coming up and everyone was going into Woking or Byfleet to get their goods and then the shops, the shops were next and we had about six hoists along there, constantly being worked and constantly breaking down and consequently being repaired, and we had motor rail dumpers – like dump trucks – going around.

I was doing the repairs and doing the servicing, everything under the sun in that little workshop over there. I liked this job because you never knew what your next job was going to be. They come from the office, 'Can you come and look at the typewriter, the typewriter's jammed up.' Well I have a look at it and clear it and see what it was. And the next time he says, 'There's a hoover in the office wants doing' and the next thing he comes in, 'Oh there's a pump down the field, he's broke down, get it out, start it up, sort it out and bring it in.' There wouldn't be a diaphragm on it, it would be the engine, anything like that. Mostly it was engine troubles – somebody put water in the fuel and it would get choked up, you'd have to clean the fuel system out, refresh, new fuel and away you go again. Oh, it was all bits and pieces, these. My responsibility was plant maintenance and repairs. That was on plant and machinery here, and that was everything, hoists, dumpers, mixers, and then also we used to run a bus from here.
William Oldall

A Lion Works truck *Ford Motor Company*

Assembly of sockets at Wandsworth Electrical, 1980s *Elsie Stranks*

The company, Wandsworth Electrical, came here in 1952, and we were the first site on Sheerwater. The knowledge was that this would be developed, yes. And for, maybe, ten or fifteen years a substantial number of people working here had come out from London. I mean, they were looking for somewhere to live after the War as well. So that's what brought them here.

This was LCC land, and we had a ninety-nine year lease on the land. And in 1970-something – it's hard to remember exactly when – the then GLC offered the leaseholders on Sheerwater (if they could find out who they were) the opportunity to purchase that. It took two years to

negotiate it. Yes, and we purchased the freehold.

Well, in those days when the company came here, it was purely switches and sockets, a variety of shapes and sizes, and we have catalogues that go actually back to 1916, that show some of the products. We were exporting to France in 1916 because we've got a French catalogue. And in the '50s, after we got here, we started to sell electrical incinerators, which were made by a company in north London which we purchased in 1968 because the owners wanted to retire, and through the '50s and '60s, and then we stopped manufacturing those incinerators just a few years ago (not the same model, I might

Press Shop at Wandsworth Electricals at Christmas, 1980s *Elsie Stranks*

add). There were two or three different sizes of incinerators.

And then, in the early '60s, we started doing work in hospitals, nurse call systems, and we're still very much into that. Of course, you can imagine then, it was relays and old fashioned type and now, of course, a lot of it's sort of digital – well, there's a little bit of hangover from analogue as well – it's sort of fairly advanced stuff. We would actually supply switches and sockets to hospitals in a large way in the '50s and '60s. Our original sort of core system was very much sort of bell-push type stuff. You know, 'Help, I want somebody.' There was no emergency systems and that's developed through the National Health Service into their broad spectrum of specifications. We're one of the three companies that have a licence granted by the NHS to supply TV telephones and very, very soon electronic patient records, through the same equipment. So we'll be, you know, ahead of the game technologically with digital systems in that area. So it's been evolutionary and we're still here.
Richard Salter

I left school on the Christmas time and I started – because in those days you only had Christmas Day and Boxing Day off – I started straight after that. I went to work wearing my socks – you know, life was so different, it was just so different. I went straight in onto the machine shop. I worked on the press section.

In those days you only had Christmas Day and Boxing Day off.

Well, when I started work, as I say, it was from 8 o'clock in the morning till 6 o'clock and we didn't have a canteen in those days. There used to be a lady that used to come and she'd make tea in a tea urn and that was at the bottom of the factory where the machine shop was and she'd boil the tea urn up and make some tea – in fact, she used to live opposite us in Henslow Way. Mrs Patterson her name was, and she was like a second mum really. She used to look after us all. The milkman used to come in and he would bring a basket with some biscuits or bits and pieces in for you that you could buy for your tea break, and we were glad of that because the temperature used to go down so low, that, at times, we used to sit with travel rugs round our legs and we even used to have pixie hoods on and gloves with no fingers in, because the metal used to be very cold.

I mean, sometimes the rain used to come through the roof and I've seen girls sit with umbrellas up.

I mean, sometimes the rain used to come through the roof and I've seen girls sit with umbrellas up but you must remember this was inside a factory that's not completely modern, although it wasn't very old, you know, it wasn't completely modernised, so what we used to do was, there used to be a chap – a young fellow – used to work in the paint shop and these boxes he used to paint, used to have to go round on like a conveyor belt to dry and they used to get hot and we used to go down and say to him, 'Can we have some of those boxes?' and we'd put them on our laps to try and keep warm, you know. But if it really got too cold, it really got below the temperatures that you could stand, it got to the point where they'd say to the Works Manager, 'Look, we've got to stop work' and, because in those days, you didn't have Personnel, there was just the one Works Manager, and he was a gentleman, a real gentleman, he used to say, 'Well, look if we get you a cup of tea to keep you warm, would you consider staying?' and people did. Mrs Patterson would put the tea on and a hot drink would come out and people would just carry on working, but, you know, you'd just do anything to keep yourself warm and I mean icicles used to be hanging around at times. But then things began to get better, as time went by, they began to have the heaters put in and things. I mean I'd even see people sit on top of their benches with an electric fire, the little old electric fires, you know, the one bar thing, and one tea break this chap was reading his newspaper and, as I say, it was before we had the canteen, he was sitting reading his newspaper and it set on fire, you know, just sitting there, didn't realise that it was going brown and browner and it set on fire.

So a few laughs went on as well, because we didn't have tannoys, there wasn't a public address or anything like that and so there was no radio. But then someone had brought in a radio, one of these old fashioned ones, and they stuck it on a little table at the end of the section and you could put that on, you'd give it a kick every now and again if it stopped, you'd give it a kick, you know, and so we got a bit of music, so we used to sing. We used to sing all day long. People would start up a song and the next one would pick up a song and it would go on like that and people would sing and sing and it was really lovely because you were working hard but you were, you know, doing it in a jolly way. Or you'd play a game of film-stars; say an initial and then the girl next to you would say, 'B.G. ... oh that's Betty Grable.' You know, you'd pass your time, with sort of things like that.

The temperature used to go down so low, that, at times, we used to sit with travel rugs round our legs and we even used to have pixie hoods on and gloves with no fingers in, because the metal used to be very cold.

We used to sing all day long. People would start up a song and the next one would pick up a song and it would go on like that and people would sing and sing and it was really lovely.

At that time, everything was under one roof and then, course it got, if there was a shortage in one place you'd be moved into another area to do something. Now I never much liked assembly work because it wasn't active enough, I preferred machine work; so I'd gone into drills, taps, milling and you know, even into the paint shop if you were needed, you sort of went where you were needed, but I preferred always to be where I could be moving about, banging or whatever, I was never much of an assembler.
Elsie Stranks

In '76, I was forty-one I think, forty-two, something like that. I used to do little cleaning jobs. I worked for this woman in Old Woking Road since my Karen was a baby and I was getting fed up of doing other people's work. Now all I had at home was Karen, she was sixteen I think, and I said to my husband one day, 'I'm going to go and find myself a job.'

He said, 'You've got a job.' I said, 'No, I'm fed up doing other people's work, I'm going to go and get a full-time job.' So he said, 'Yeah, yeah, yeah, alright.' Well, I went to the Wandsworth – it was easier to get a job then, I'm going back '76. So I went over to Wandsworth and, of course, my mum used to work there, my sister used to work there. I got a job and he said, 'When do you want to start?' I said, 'Monday,' and he said, 'Would you like to go on inspection?' I said, 'I'm not worried what I do.' I came home here and said, 'I've got a job.' 'Huh?' I said, 'I got a job, I start at Wandsworth Electrical on Monday.' 'Oh yeah, give you three months,' sort of thing. Well, I was there twenty-four years. I retired three years ago at the age of sixty-five and I went and worked on inspection and worked me way up from there and I had my own three benches. I used to do a lot of this inspection, big units for hospitals and prisons. I got quite a good job there, very good job.
Joyce Gee

Most parents said to you when you went to work that you stay at that job because it's going to be a good reference and you didn't jump in and out of work quite so easily whereas now even that's changed now.

Yes, I just felt comfortable there and, of course, in those days, like I suppose everybody else my age group, most parents said to you when you went to work that you stay at that job because it's going to be a good reference and you didn't jump in and out of work quite so easily whereas now even that's changed now. Now it would be the more jobs you'd had... I just felt that I fitted in there and it was just part of my life, you know, used to go down there every day, go in, clock in – we had the old clock-ins then– put your card in, just bang the handle down and away you'd go. Of course, then we saw the coming of the canteen and that was absolute – oh – that was wonderful that was, the thought of having a canteen; and we had a lady starting, a Mrs Higgs – she's from Sheerwater as well. It was mostly Sheerwater people. She went out and she chose all the cups and saucers, but the cups and saucers were for management, the factory people you could have just ordinary cups, you know, but management there were green cups and green saucers, which us young people thought, 'Pooh, well what's wrong with us?' but that was life, just life went on.

Christmas we'd have our little get-togethers, each section would take their little party piece in, their sandwiches or their sausage rolls, each one would do something and each section would either take in their little record player or a little radio and you'd be within your own little bit and that was your get-together before you packed up for Christmas, remembering that we were working Christmas Eve up to finishing time, which was six o'clock. And there's many a time I've known people that they forgot to go and collect their meat out the butcher's and it's still been in the butcher's and they've been, you know... But people were happy, well at least they seemed to be happy and make the best out of it all.
Elsie Stranks

There was a lot of community spirit within Sheerwater. There still is an allotment in Sheerwater but in the '50s and '60s Wandsworth Electrical presented prizes for the allotment.

Not many people had cars. There were lots more buses around the place but people didn't travel very far. So there was a lot of community spirit within Sheerwater. There still is an allotment in Sheerwater but in the '50s and '60s Wandsworth Electrical presented prizes for the allotment. I don't know whether it was the largest onion or the smallest bean.

There was always a very active social club and part of that social club was sports but that went in and out of favour. I mean the '50s and '60s were very big cricketing times. The '70s we had our– as far as I know – the first sort of football team, which seemed to do quite well as well in the odd league. And then that faded. It didn't take many people to retire or leave or break a leg or something before you didn't have enough footballers. And then we went back into cricket and we're still in cricket, in various leagues.We always had an annual dinner, which I think started sometime in the '50s. Certainly the first one I went to was in 1971, which was at The Burford Bridge Hotel and they went to different places. Sometimes there was live music, sometimes there was a comedian. Sometimes there's this, that and the other but it was all organised by the Sports and Social Club. It was not organised by the company. The company, in the early days, contributed, if I remember rightly, half a bottle of wine per person. Or something like that, as opposed to a lump sum.

If you look over the last thirty years there were many, many outings and transport was provided and all the rest of it but, nowadays, if you want to take people to the coast they've already been, yesterday, you see? So you don't have to hire a bus to take people to Brighton or to take people to Eastbourne because they've just been. Nearly everybody is totally mobile. And so that has made a big, big difference to the social life.
Richard Salter

I started at Efco's on Sheerwater as a junior clerk, just generally filing, going and getting the cheese rolls and the tea for the men that I worked with, because it was in the Estimating Department and, gradually, learning to type and things like that. And the lady I worked for suggested I should go to night school because then I could work my way up to a copy typist. So I enrolled at Woking College and went there and learnt to type. Which I did, on one of the old typewriters, the Underwood's. And I worked my way up and, eventually, I ended up as a copy typist because the men in them days used to write out what they wanted you to type, not machines.
Janet Hicks

After eight years I was made redundant because they closed that building, and when they closed, they said, 'You can have anything you like, take anything you like.' What did I have? Oh, a big saucepan and that big teapot. Don't think I had very much did I?

It would be the mid-'60s I started work. I started work in Efco's, in the canteen there, doing rolls and serving tea to the people in the factory and I stayed there about eight years. They used to pay for the rolls as they had them and then their tea, well I used to go round on a Friday, very very quickly, while they were having their tea break, to collect their tea money. I had a book, you know, and those who didn't pay, only used to pay at the weekend, and then I used to get their money on a Friday, for their teas. So they must have paid for their rolls as they went along.

After eight years I was made redundant because they closed that building, and when they closed, they said, 'You can have anything you like, take anything you like.' What did I have? Oh, a big saucepan and that big teapot, still got it to this day. Every time we have a big party, or a big get-together, such as a funeral we've had recently and that, and then we take the teapot up, you know. So I had the teapot, I had a big saucepan which I boil my tea-cloths up in occasionally. Don't think I had very much did I?
Pat Bell

When the Sorbo turned out you knew, because everybody that got on the bus or whatever, they had white eyelashes, from the dust, and those people used to work ever so hard in there. It was a big firm but they worked very hard but you could smell the smell of rubber.
Elsie Stranks

I went to work for Sorbo's for a little while, I think I only done part time there while the children were at school. I used to jazz balls. Little spongy balls – well I used to work in the jazzing department there. All these colours like green, red, blue, all these colours come down and you used to have all these balls on these little pins, loads of them, you pick them up and you just jazz them through and they all came out all different colour balls, like red and yellow and blue and green.

They were just play balls. I don't think you see that sort of thing today, I'm going back a few years now, forty years, it's got to be forty-odd years. That's what I used to do there.
Joyce Gee

There was a factory here called Sorbo Polymers. I got job there and I worked there for about one and a half years or something and then that closed down. My wife's uncle was working there and he told me that there is a vacancy there so I want to come and try. He brought the forms for me and I fill it. So I went for an interview and he said, 'OK, you can start.'

I was working on the machine in a moulding, a machine operator there making these rubber screens for Volvo cars. The screen rubbers, the windscreen rubbers, the rubbers that go round the edge of the windscreen. I was joining them in the machine. Putting them in some rubber capsules and it was moulds. I think it was five for each operator. Five machines so you start from one mould and then it needs to go slowly and then in the end there is a complete screen. Every operator was responsible for that.

The factory closed down. They went to somewhere else, I don't know where they moved. After a few months I found a job in James Walker, Lion Works, just around the corner, next to the Mosque. I worked there for eight years.
Deran Shah

When the Sorbo turned out you knew, because everybody that got on the bus or whatever, they had white eyelashes, from the dust, and those people used to work ever so hard in there.

I went to work for Ken Wood, the mixer people[4] , when he first came to Woking. It was in Goldsworth Road. I was his only office staff and he had, I don't know, half a dozen chaps in the factory, I suppose, which was at the very back, ran right down to the other road. He started off by making toasters and from that it sort of started to grow and grow and grow, and then he made his mixers. I did everything really, if I remember. I did his letters and did his vast payroll and I could tell you all sorts of things, but I mustn't, because... I must not, I must not! I was there two years and I did enjoy it. Then eventually I left and after that they moved – he moved down to Havant, or somewhere I think.
Greta Ledger

4 The company itself is, of course, Kenwood. (Ed.)

Aerial photo of James Walker *James Walker*

James Walker's internal fire and medical services *James Walker*

I was on the old fire brigade. It was a very nice job. We did absolutely nothing and we got paid well for it. We used to start at seven. We used to sit around all day, watching telly, hoping that the bells would go down for a fire but we didn't get very many.

James Walker and Company. Very nice company it was too. Well, when I first started there must have been about two thousand people worked there and then, when I finished, there was only a couple... three hundred. So that shows you how downhill it had gone. It was a good company. They made packings, jointings and 'o' rings and all sorts of stuff. It started off with an old bloke called James Walker, who come from London and he started off by making greasy string for ships' propeller glands. He used to sell this greasy string on a barrow and that's how he started off. Made himself a fortune, very clever.

I was on the old fire brigade. It was a very nice job. We did absolutely nothing and we got paid well for it. We used to start at seven. We used to sit around all day, watching telly, hoping that the bells would go down for a fire but we didn't get very many. We didn't have an official lunch break but we had loads of time off anyway so it didn't matter. Then we used to come home again at seven. So, very good.

When I first joined there was three crews of ten men each so that was thirty. And then there was what they called a Station Officer and a Chief Fire Officer, so that was thirty-two. We had two fire appliances. We had an ambulance because we used to run the ambulance as well. We had to do First Aid. And we had what they called a patrol car because we used to have to go and patrol four outside factories. We was like a proper little fire brigade. Yep, we had all the stuff.

In the latter years, when we changed the shift pattern, we used to work two days, two nights and four off and we used to get about seven weeks a year holiday. So, all in all, we worked about a hundred and twenty six days in the year. So that's four months of the year we used to work. It was really good.

Major accidents? Not major accidents, no. We had a big fire once that burnt down one of the parts of the factory. It started off as a little fire. A bloke grabbed a bucket thinking it was water and threw it on it and it turned out to be spirit so the next thing you know – whoosh! Half the building's gone.

We did do First Aid, yeah, we used to do a First Aid course, three days. Very good it was too, with the old St John's Ambulance. I didn't like it much, it wasn't my thing but it was easy enough.

A bloke grabbed a bucket thinking it was water and threw it on it and it turned out to be spirit so the next thing you know – whoosh! Half the building's gone.

We used to have some quite – well – not bad accidents. I was called down one day to take a bloke to hospital and he'd caught one of his fingers in a machine and it ripped his finger off. It was horrible. When we were going the nurse said to me, 'Don't leave this behind.' And she give me a kidney bowl with a bit of blue paper on the top. When I lifted it up there's this bloke's finger inside! Oh, it was horrid. And we had another bloke who was cutting sheets of rubber-type cork sheeting with a big sharp knife and he drew it right across his thigh and cut it wide open. He went like that and he just kept going, straight over his leg. And it was deep but there was hardly any blood. It was just like slicing open a lump of beef.

We had a few break-ins. There was a bloke broke in one night and he was huge. He was built like a gorilla and he was trying to cart away a safe. You know how heavy safes are? This bloke got in and he picked this little safe up and he carted it away, smashed it open and there was nothing in it. Usually it had money in it but this time it had nothing. But, anyway, someone heard him and they went to look for him and he disappeared but, as they're hunting around, someone shone these lights up into the rafters and the bloke was up there hiding up in the roof. Terrible.

The social club, it had a bar. They had a nice little lounge and then, if there was a dance up there, they used to clear one of the dining rooms, make a nice dance hall. It was good.

They had a top dining hall and a bottom one and we used to be in the bottom and upstairs was the sort of like managers. And then one separate end used to be the directors. So they didn't sort of mix in with the hoi polloi. You know what I mean? They just stuck to theirselves.

On the Walker's site itself there was sort of like two factories on one site. You had James Walker and Company and then you had Flexible Cork Company. God knows how many buildings but it was a big site.

It started off as The College of Oriental Arts. I've seen the pictures and it had huge great gardens that run straight down to the railway. They had the boardroom up there. That was a lovely little building that was.

The Boardroom? It looked very posh when you went in it and it was all wooden panels and had these little stained glass windows. But the wood panelling when they was knocking Walker's down, they ripped the panelling off and what we thought was oak panelling turned out to be old packing crates. It used to be a place where they used to build aircraft during the War. Well, the First World War anyway. The packing crates – they used to line the walls, but it looked good. It had a big

Board table. There was a stuffed lion in there. There was a polar bear on the floor, polar bear skin. It had all sorts in there. The logo from The Lion Works, the old lion, but the poor old thing it had to go in the end because it was getting all moth-eaten and it was in a terrible state.

At the time it must have been one of the biggest employers in Woking, if not the biggest because, like I say, when I first went there there was a fair old few hundred used to work there. They used to go streaming out at night. Literally thousands of them streaming out of there. In the end

The boardroom at
James Walker
James Walker

it used to be just a little trickle going out. Shame really because they've moved most of it away now.

They've gone up to Cockermouth in Cumbria. And they've gone down to Tavis-tock and some other place, down the West Country. Because it's cheaper I suppose, they wanted to save money like everybody else.

They had a big sale. They took every-thing out of there. All the old machinery which must have been eighty year old from when the factory first started. It was really old stuff. They dismantled it all and

an Indian guy come in and bought most of the factory out and shipped it all off to India. He must have made a fortune, that bloke.

David Baldwin

It had a big Board table. There was a stuffed lion in there. There was a polar bear on the floor, polar bear skin. It had all sorts in there.

Because it was so noisy we had a thing that looked just like a sentry box in the corner of the office when the phone rang we would get up and go into this sentry box, which had acoustic padding round it.

My first job was taking orders over the telephone. It was extremely difficult because I didn't know anything about the products. Because it was so noisy it was very, very difficult to hear what people were saying. They were ringing up from all over the country in various accents, wanting to place orders for these products. It was rather amusing really. Because it was so noisy we had a thing that looked just like a sentry box in the corner of the office where we were sitting and when the phone rang we would get up and go into this sentry box, which sort of had acoustic padding round it. We would listen and write the orders down. Most of it was for ships, 'cause Walker's made lots of stuff for shipping and we had a service where they could ring up at a certain time of the day and we would guarantee to send the product out the next day. So we had to make sure that we'd got all the details right and that it could be done for the next day. We had no headphones. It was just an old black bakelite-type phone in your ear that rang and it had a dial. And there was a switchboard between us and them – lots of girls who worked on a switchboard – but they had headphones and they plugged things in. Lots of local girls. Some of them were very nice and some of them were not so nice. Did feel a little bit vulnerable 'cause there weren't many

blokes spare and they knew the ways of the world really. You could get yourself into trouble really if you said things out of place. I quite enjoyed office work.

They needed somebody on this section called the Progress, which was a small group of us, again mostly girls, under a manager who was quite bad tempered. He always seemed to be bad tempered and the idea there was that we were trying to find out all of the orders in the factory. We were very, very busy at that time. The company was working twenty-four hours a day and had lots of orders and the deliveries dates were very, very long and people kept ringing up or writing in wanting to know when they were going to get their goods. So we had to find out and tell them when they were going to get their goods. And they were usually not happy because it's already late and it was going to be even later. So you're under a lot of pressure and everybody was pretty uptight. Especially the manager, who was quite, as I've said, bad tempered. And the girls used to say to me, you know, 'Can you give him this?' Because some mess had been created, you know? Some mistake. 'I can't go and see him. I'll wet myself if I have to go and see him.' So I used to have to go and see him. And he'd go red and get very excited. He was sort of like a bomb about to go off, without warning. One of his little party tricks was, he would bound out of his office and he had a sort of hammer or mallet thing and he would bang it on the nearest girl's desk and shout, 'Come on you girls, quieten down!' Of course, the one sitting at the desk would practically die of shock.

It was a very old fashioned sort of set-up. The Managing Director used to address us over the loudspeaker system. He'd give us a little chat and we'd all sit there listening to him. Well, he'd talk about

One of his little party tricks was, he would bound out of his office and he had a mallet thing and he would bang it on the nearest girl's desk and shout, 'Come on you girls, quieten down!' The one sitting at the desk would practically die of shock.

When I first went to work there in 1954, there were about two thousand people there and when I left there were a hundred.

how the company was going and how we'd all got to work hard and we'd got to honour our delivery dates. What we really wanted to know is how many weeks bonus we were going to get in the summer and Christmas.

I worked in the factory sometimes. They had these big intermixers and some had rollers which were going round with rubber on and there were safety devices but if they dropped their knife in they'd make a grab for it. It was highly dangerous and then one poor man was on the intermix and I think he dropped his broom in and made a grab for it and he lost his fingers or just the ends of them.

They mixed rubber, whether it's tyres or a mixture of things. You've got the sort of basic natural rubber – or, more likely, it will be synthetic rubber – and you add compounds and chemicals to that to get the effect you want. I mean for tyres they stick in loads of carbon black to give the wear capabilities but then there's also sulphur and anti-oxidants. It's a fairly precise science, of designing the rubber to do the job that it's specifically for. It wouldn't be the same sort of thing for the mat that you stood on because that would be quite a cheap product really. Absolutely full of cork but it wasn't going to be bent around

much. It had to obviously be resistant to oil but it was not going to move. They made gaskoid jointing, a foul smelling paper stuff which was dipped into a chemical for use on carburettors. A little thin paper gasket that used to go between the head of the carburettor and the bottom could have been a gaskoid jointing. It would withstand soaking in petrol and make a reasonable joint and not fall to pieces.

They didn't move many of the people that actually worked at Woking up to Cockermouth. They obtained a factory which was empty up in Cockermouth and they took a couple of key people from Woking, one on the production side and one as the sort of Director of Operations and they recruited people. There were masses of people out of work at that time up there because there wasn't much industry around. There were some shoe factories and steel works which were going through troubled times. Walker's recruited and trained the people to do the work, really replicating what had been done at Woking but with more efficient machinery. That gradually grew and took over the work from Woking. It was originally opened to boost production and try and help us to keep up. But, of course, when quiet times came along then they wound down the Woking end.

When I first went to work there in 1954, there were about two thousand people there and when I left there were a hundred. They were all office staff but they're not there either now.
Martin Bowman

I worked there twenty-six years. When I had completed twenty-five years I received a television as a gift.

I went to work at Walker's and I was there for twenty-seven years. I was one of the inspectors, the end-of-line quality control and I was team leader there for fifteen years. It was a very responsible job, because they did all aeroplane seals and gaskets, they did seals for the North Sea oil. All these things had to be looked at for faults and measured, because if they weren't the right size accidents might have happened.

They had special gauges, Verniers, a measuring gauge and micrometers. If the seals were big, we had to look at drawings because we used to get a lot of split ones. So if they were split they were no good – or if we used to get a lot with dirt in the material after moulding.

Every time a new job came in a new mould was created. I used to sample the moulds, then sampled the first three seals on a dynascope. It's like an x-ray machine – it gives you all the sizes and records it and that was like a certificate for that mould. We sampled the first three seals on a dynascope, then they went to press.
Calogera Morreale

You will not believe me but there were French, Germans but no Pakistanis at that time. There were many, many Italians. They came by the cartload! Every day there were new people who had been called by their relations or friends who had found work here. Gradually people bought their own houses. For instance mine cost £2,500 at that time, in 1965 or '66.

In 1963 I did all the different jobs with machines. They made rubber gaskets for trains, for ships, for aeroplanes, for wheels and brakes. Lion Works made all sorts of different things. I worked there twenty-six years. When I had completed twenty-five years I received a television as a gift.
Antonio Falsetta

I worked in what they called the grease shop. West Works was the official name but everybody else called it the grease shop because it was nothing but grease and graphite. We used to go home dirty and greasy. There were presses and machines – large, medium, small machines, then they had these presses where you made packing. You'd make it up into what we would call rings. They were put into steel things and then you'd press them together. You had to make sure it was the right size. Everything was expertly examined because they had to be dead right. If there were rejects they'd just sling them back, no good. They had to be cleaned off so that it was all smooth because they went in tanks, they went on ships etc..

They'd have 'Music While You Work' on and that was lovely, you know, you was all singing away there while we were working.
Cynthia Reed

At work in James Walker *James Walker*

There was a chap who worked for James Walker who was in the army. When the War finished, he went into the Luftwaffe place in Germany and to everybody's amazement, there was a full set of up-to-date plans of James Walker's, which he brought back to Woking. James Walker's people have always wondered who was giving the Germans the information of everything they did at James Walker's. *Philip Ledger*

They'd have 'Music While You Work' on and that was lovely, you know, you was all singing away there while we were working.

James Walker West works – braided packing ring section, c. 1950 *The Lightbox*

I started in the James Walker asbestos shop, grinding up old asbestos which, when you think of it, would not be allowed now.

I started in the James Walker asbestos shop, grinding up old asbestos which, when you think of it, would not be allowed now. We used rubber, asbestos and a solvent to mix it and then you made it in sheet form which made packings which went between two metal surfaces to provide the actual packing.

There was notices up, very small ones, saying that asbestos was hazardous. You could wear a mask, but we didn't really know about it. When I came back from the Royal Navy, I knew about it then because the Navy used asbestos – for health reasons we all wore masks. We found out the various types of asbestos; blue asbestos which came from Canada was the killer. I found out where all the different asbestos came from – Australia, Italy, South Africa – and the qualities of them. Later on in my life people started coming to me for my knowledge about it. It's not dangerous in a rock form but it's when they crush it and tease it – dust gets in the air – that it's bad.

I'd got made Leading Hand and then I got made up to Charge Hand. If a lorry came in, you decided how you were going to have it unloaded and the blokes who were going to do it and where they did it. Because in those days we never had forklifts and we used to carry really heavy loads. Some of them used to weigh up to five hundredweight and I and another chap, we used to be able to carry one of those between us – we were pretty hard in those days. They never had a union for years. But James Walker brought in a production bonus, it was very good. We used to get six to eight weeks bonus at the August holidays, which was two weeks shut down and Christmas. Originally in the old days, pre-War, we used to pack up at 5.30 on Christmas Eve and we were back the day after Boxing Day and at that time it used to be 7am start and if we were over three minutes late we used to lose our holiday money. That's how tough it was and there was no argument. If they came along and said, 'You're out' – which has happened – you were out straight away. But then when the unions came in, they said 'No, we're going to spread that over the year.' The unions were probably correct in their way, but we liked it as it was.

People like my father used to get a pound a week extra for being Londoners, because they had the job knowledge. If the locals were on £2, 10 shillings to £3 a week, they were on £3, 10 shillings and it was because we moved down from London.

We were like a glorified ship's chandlers. We provided everything that was necessary to keep the engines going on ships. Then it was the oil rigs and we had to do all the joints and everything for them. Aberdeen really built up and everything was hurry, hurry. If a breakdown came, it cost us money. We used to have big things like the steel works in Wales, where we used to provide all the Walker seals for the rollers there.

You didn't throw away a piece of string more than four inches, you saved everything.

Going back many years, of course, the steel company in Wales said, 'If our production line stops, it's £1,000 a minute' – a huge amount. So we used to have these rollers with the water seals put in – we actually had people in the steel company in Wales who belonged to James Walker's, just to keep it all going twenty-four hours a day. So everything was in a hurry, like the oil rigs. At the end if you have something go wrong, the Americans could get it in quicker than you could get it up to Aberdeen and across and that's how it went. But, of course, as the ships disappeared the rolling mills went, the coalmines, everything just went.

The earlier workers were engineers really and they knew where all the packings had to go and why and they developed them. We were always known as the ones who came down from London, because, I don't know if they knew it in those days, but people like my father used to get a pound a week extra for being Londoners, because they had the job knowledge, which was a big, big bonus really. If the locals were on £2, 10 shillings to £3 a week, they were on £3, 10 shillings and it was because we moved down from London, but because they had the know-how and all. They didn't get automatically get made up in charge or anything like that, it was just the know-how of how they used to do it. I remember Mr Cook, if he picked up a bit of string and he used to think it was more than four inches long, you didn't throw away a piece of string more than four inches, you saved everything.

There was bad days in the '20s and '30s, and we were living from hand to mouth. But the War made us. Everything went on production, day shift, night shift, three shifts, everything, money was no object.

There was bad days in the '30s, as you know, '20s and '30s, when things did go downhill and we were living from hand to mouth. It sounds terrible to say it, but the War made us. Everything went on production, day shift, night shift, three shifts, everything, money was no object in some ways.
Fred Woodhouse

The canteen at James Walker *James Walker*

The workers' canteen was in the social club, it was big like a village hall. There were things like dartboards on the walls and then there were all these tables, trestles and chairs.

The Lion Works was a big employer in the area. It was a huge site that borders onto the railway line where most of the people worked. At lunch time, when the hooter went for lunch, they would just swarm out of the gates. It was just like watching ants and they swarmed to the bike parks. Very few people had cars, and the road would be black for ten minutes while they all got on their bikes and went home to eat, because it was cheaper.

At lunch time, when the hooter went for lunch, they would just swarm out of the gates.

There was a canteen there but most people seemed to go elsewhere and then back in one hour and you had to clock on. I worked there when I left school. You'd got a few white collar workers amongst them but mainly they were on the shop floor making packings and jointings for heavy machinery, trains, buses and that kind of thing. Covered in graphite and slippery but quite fascinating.

The Directors' canteen was laid out with white napery and serviettes. That would be one world and round the corner was the works canteen which was a different world altogether.

I'm a shorthand typist and so I worked in the office. I was only seventeen or eighteen. But Lion Works itself was very paternalistic. There was the Director and his family worked there, his daughter and one of the sons. There were a whole hierarchy of the Sales Directors. At Christmas, they gave us Christmas parties. We went to the boss's house and so forth. But the day-to-day running, the working situation at the Lion Works, was you clocked on at 8.30 and everyone had to clock on. You worked until 10am and there was a tea break of quarter of an hour. At 12.30. the hooter blew, everyone went out, the hooter blows again 1.25 to tell you half past one is the time; two hooters – clock on. The whole neighbourhood could hear it because it needed to get to the surrounding area where everyone worked and lived. If you were in bed asleep! We lived about five hundred yards I think from the Lion Works – you could hear it clearly from our house.

There was the Directors' canteen which was laid out with white napery and serviettes. That was in the main part of the building, the old college. That would be one world and round the corner was the works canteen which was a different world altogether. The workers' canteen was in the social club, it was big like a village hall. There were things like dartboards on the walls and then there were all these tables, trestles and chairs. There was the row of hot plates and women who were serving out the food. So there would be a choice of egg, baked beans and mash or sometimes there would be mince and mash and cabbage – very basic food.
Barbara Beaumont

I left school and the following week I thought, 'I'll have to go and get a job.' I eventually landed up at Lion Packing Works. I worked there for one week.

I left school and the following week I thought, 'I'll have to go and get a job.' I eventually landed up at Lion Packing Works. I worked there for one week. I didn't like that one little bit. It was making packing with asbestos string, which I don't think would have been allowed today because the asbestos dust was floating all over the place. The machine I worked had a lot of bobbins which were sort of weaving this stuff into a sort of a rope and there was about eight bobbins loaded with this asbestos string which wove round into this string packing which was then squashed into a square shape. I stuck that for a week.
Bert Hollis

Back home I worked for myself. Our own business; so when I work in the factory I couldn't take someone's orders. I forced myself to work there but I was always looking forward to do my own business. But any business that you do here, you need lots of capital and a place, and what you call a support from the family, but my children were very young and I tried for some time to have a sub-postmaster, post business, Post Office. I thought that this needed lots of effort and also I don't want to put my wife or my children in to... to force them to help me out and give them hard times, so it's better that I worked for myself. The taxi is a business that is just connected with me. Not with my family; and so, if my wife or my children need time from me, if there is a thing that they are going to go to, I can take them. I can give them time but I don't need their time to help me with my business.
Deran Shah

Back home I worked for myself. Our own business; so when I work in the factory I couldn't take someone's orders. I forced myself to work there but I was always looking forward to do my own business.

I seen the job in Creators, I went to apply there. It was so hard in those days and I was looking... I wasn't that good really at filling in the form generally and I had gone and spoken to him. He said, 'There's a lot of people.' I said, 'How many people have come?' 'Forty-five people applied for the job but you are the better and fitter one.' I was very slim and very fit looking.

And then a couple of days later he write me a letter and he said, 'Come and start work on Monday.' I worked there five years. On my shift I was in charge after two or three years. Very good on the job. I required other bits like forklift driving and everything.

They were making plaster covers, working in compound, making the pipes and everything from that. There was the powder coming in different bags and different bits and we were mixing the powder and oil together and making chips, small chip things.

After five years, that factory was closed. That place we was working and the whole place was closed; so I come out and start looking for a job again. '86, and it was a very hard time again. I didn't find a job. At one time I was going to leave this place, you know? I was going to go. Because this area was expensive. I owned the house but I thought, 'No job.' I was going to go to the Midlands, Burton-on-Trent.

I stayed there one week and looking for job there as well but I didn't get anything. And, after a week, I just decide to come back. Then I did not go on the dole again. I bought the car and start a taxi. I did get some redundancy money of course. Fifteen, sixteen hundred. I had some savings as well. I think I bought a car for nine hundred or something like that.

Between now and the station, generally, we just wait in the queue, line by line, and then the others come to you and ask you if they're going only a short distance and they just get in. If they are going the long distance they ask you the price and if you give them the right price, they take it.

I had a person come to my car and he was going to Sutton in Surrey and he didn't have no money on him. No, he only had £10 on him and he swear on his mother's life and all that to say that I can pay you the other end. And I get out the other end and I stopped my car. He stopped at a very big house near and I just notice he's going to go into that house and then I see him walking the other way. And I come out from the car and he had the legs... He's gone. And the fare was for £45 and he only pay me £10. That's the worst one I ever had.
Mohammed Afsar

Oh, I done a thousand things. Initially I went into a Merchant Navy Training School, I wanted to join the Merchant Navy and I went to training school in Kent but, again, had a good home life, I think I stayed there two months and then decided it wasn't for me. Then I was lorry driving for quite a few years, I got a Class 1, driving artics., I was a bingo caller in a seaside bingo for three years.
Paul Allen

I was nineteen when I set up the business. Well, it was a boy's situation, it was risky – I wouldn't do it now. But we had this little job, me and my cousin, we had this little job, building and landscaping and then a little of the time, we weren't doing much, but a little bit of the time after two or three years, we got established and we had about eight other people working for us.

Well, because I worked two years in swimming pools. Obviously swimming pools is building and landscaping, although you don't actually build houses, but you build walls around. Even we used to build inside, indoor swimming pools and when they were outside, you did the landscape as well. So that two years I learnt quite a lot, I'm a very good learner actually when I see something.

My cousin was working in a hospital, St Peter's. I think he was working in the mortuary room for about two or three years and, because he was on shift work, part time, he was going doing gardens and things like that. So, basically, he had a couple of gardens maintenance kind of thing and we found this little job and he said, 'Shall we try and establish something?' and I said, 'Yes, okay.' When you're young, you don't really think of what the consequences could be, but it turned out to be all right.

We just started with maintenance and you only need a machine, a mower sort of thing. He had a small van that he was going to work with, a very small van and that's how we started. Once we got the money together, we bought a truck and a bigger van but, at the time, we didn't have any money anyway. We stayed together for nineteen years in this business.
Pino Aina

Luigi Alighieri, hairdresser, in his salon in Victoria Way, 1978 *Luigi Alighieri*

Well, I carried on with the band. I didn't have a job. I was unemployed for some time, which was a total disgrace being Italian and you were supposed to go and work. So, my mother said, 'Right. You've got to go out today and get a job.' And she said, 'I think you should do hairdressing.' So I said, 'Right, OK.' Which I really didn't want to do at all. But I got a job in a place called Robert Christopher's, which is round the back of the station. The wrong side or the right side depending on which way you want to have a look at it. Because it was built the wrong way round, wasn't it? And that's the posh end. It was on the posh end. So, I went to work there. Didn't really like it and still carried on playing with the band all the time.
Enzo Esposito

Woking is a new town or was a new town with the coming of the railways – yes, it had opportunity and that's why people came. It was exciting.

Edward Miller had the first departmental store, as far as I understand, in Woking. The girls lived in. There were about twelve of them and they had a housekeeper to look after them and Mum came up to train as a window dresser from Worthing, because that's where my folks on my mother's side all originate from: the Sussex Downs and Chichester. So she came up in 1916 presumably and Dad had gone to the War, the First World War, he was in the Royal Corps of Signals, and had survived the War and came back to Woking you see, and saw my mother in the window, dressing the window and fell in love with her and they were married in 1922. So that's how we started here, it's purely as Woking is a new town or was a new town with the coming of the railways – yes, it had opportunity and that's why people came. It was exciting.
Pamela Green

I left school in the August; well, I didn't leave school because my mother said she wouldn't let me leave unless I'd got a situation, and, apparently, a Miss Smith who had been with Gammons for years came down and said to my mother, 'You have a daughter, I believe, leaving school, or of school leaving age,' so mother said, 'Yes,' so she said, 'Well, we wish to have an apprentice and we wonder whether she would be interested.' Well, of course you didn't have Careers – people didn't come to school and ask you – and I really didn't know. I knew I didn't want to go into service and of course unless your parents could pay, you couldn't learn typing or shorthand. Any rate, so I had to go up to the back of the station, to this gentleman, to his private house with my mother and he was in the garden and he seemed a very, you know, a severe man, and he asked me if I would be interested, so I said I thought I would. He said, 'Very well, you start on the Monday, 24th September.'

She said 'Why didn't you sit for the Grammar School?' But my parents couldn't have afforded it and nobody pushed, nobody said.

And I remember I had to tell the mistress I was leaving, you see. She then said to me, 'Why didn't you sit for the Grammar School?' But of course, my parents couldn't have afforded it and nobody pushed, nobody said. I suppose they knew you wouldn't be able to get there, and on the Monday my mother went up to the shop and she bought some black sateen, that was a shiny material, and I had a black overall, long sleeves with a pocket, which she made. You had to have a handkerchief, a pair of scissors with a blunted end, and a pencil, and that was all you were supposed to have in your pocket. And I remember my father wouldn't allow me to take any money with me at all. He said, 'You don't need it, you live near work, then if there's any bother at all, you've no money. If you have, where did you get it from?' Because we were brought up then that what was our own was our own, but you didn't take what didn't belong to you, or unless you had paid for it.
Ada Green

I left school on the Friday and I started work on the Monday. I had a weekend off. In fact, I was worse off then than my Saturday job.

I just walked into places that I liked the look of. And I walked into Woking News and Mail, I walked into Moldram and Wilson's, which was the estate agents and County Press. And they all – again, I'm not being big-headed – but they all give me a chance to start there.

Now, all my friends were having all of the six weeks holiday off. They left school and they had six weeks off but my Mum needed money so I didn't even have a day off. I left school on the Friday and I started work on the Monday. I had a weekend off. In fact, I was worse off then than my Saturday job. By the time I paid my Mum and sent Mandy her bus fares... I did get a bit bitter... So I got another job. A shitty, horrible job (excuse my French) in the ABC Cinema, as an usherette. Half past five finish at Moldram and Wilson and guess what time I started as an usherette? Half past five. I didn't have wings. So I did explain that. They allowed that. 'You can come in at a quarter to six.' And then I worked till half past eleven at night. Three nights a week at fifteen years old. And then I worked at the golf course. At the end there, I had about five jobs.
Sandra Thurling

Interior of Robinsons, c.1960 *David Robinson*

My father started the Robinsons shop in Woking. In 1937 he bought P N Edwards, which was in the High Street, and sadly he died in 1946, and my mother then took on and ran the stores. And we bought a number of other businesses, including over a period of time Bennet's, which was opposite Robinsons in Chertsey Road, and Owen's, which was in Commercial Way. We then bought the shops adjoining us, which were Maynard's, Pocock's and Farmer's the shoe store. And having bought them, we demolished Robinsons, we moved out into Edwards', Bennet's and Owen's, and rebuilt a five-floor modern building with a restaurant on the top, and we traded from there until the town centre was built in Wolsey Place.

Trade then moved out of Chertsey Road, and we converted the top of the building into offices and in due course moved out to Commercial Way. We moved out to Commercial Way because we were then employing third generation staff and they had given us tremendous loyalty and we owed them loyalty, and so those who wanted a job carried on in Commercial Way until we finally closed. But we also bought a store, John Marsh in Horsham and Bobbies in Bognor. They were related to the big Bobbies which were bought by Debenhams, but this was one that escaped, and we've only just recently closed all our retail businesses. So although I do work now it is very sporadic and it's only looking after the properties.
David Robinson

We moved out to Commercial Way because we were then employing third generation staff and they had given us tremendous loyalty and we owed them loyalty, and so those who wanted a job carried on in Commercial Way until we finally closed.

My father opened up a boys' shop in 36, Chertsey Road and moved that to 21, Chobham Road and opened up a tailoring shop at 29, Chobham Road and then in 1934, he opened up a shop in Reigate – Bell Street, Reigate. It was known as Sydney Bailey – Sydney Bailey and the Boys' Shop. He started the business in 1919 and he retired to Torquay in 1938, so he had nineteen years in business and left me carrying the can.

I had an uncle, which was my mother's brother, and he was quite brilliant in engineering and it's in the family. That's why I feel that, in many ways, I was in the wrong trade but I carried on from what my father started. My brother went to university and my sister went to university, but I just came into the business and got on with it. We used to supply all the uniforms for Allen House and the Boys' Grammar School, which is now the police station and a lot of the schools round.

I can see from the word go, I was programmed to go into the business. Because

I can remember quite distinctly when we were living in Chobham Road, my father got quite friendly with the man who produced a magazine called The Efficiency Magazine, and this was all about the efficiency of running business and it bored me stiff. But he used to come down to the house and talk to my father and talk to me, but it didn't make much impression on me I'm afraid. I was much happier reading *Modern Boy*, I think it was called, a magazine in those days which was about the more practical things in life.

I feel that, in many ways, I was in the wrong trade but I carried on from what my father started. My brother went to university and my sister went to university, but I just came into the business and got on with it.

The interiors of the shops were wooden because my father and I made a lot of the fixtures. I can remember spending hours making drawers for putting shirts and things in at home, whilst my father was up at the business – on a fretsaw machine which was run on treadles. I made a lot of those and then, as the years went by, I refitted Chertsey Road and did all the fixtures in there and I closed the tailoring shop and brought that up to Chertsey Road and I made all the fixtures for that upstairs, which was quite a job when I think of it and then over at Reigate, I had that extended and then I extended it again with the aid of a friend of mine who did the brickwork and I did all the joists and all the rest of it for the roof and put the roof on and got it all tarmacked over. So that was really, in many ways, more interesting than running the business.

The counters were glazed so you could put the stuff on display in them and there was a window display and I can remember on one occasion, I was in the window and I was changing an electric fitting and I'd turned the mains off and put the scissors through the wires and it welded the scissors together and fortunately, it didn't throw me out of the window. Somebody had connected the wires to the windows on the wrong side of the fuse box, but how I survived that I don't know. I kept the scissors for some time because they were just welded together. I had to get the Woking Electric Company, which was then in existence, to come and put a new mains fuse in.

Most of our customers were in about a five or ten mile radius, something like that. Most of them were in Woking, St Johns, Hook Heath. We had a lot of customers up at Hook Heath, there was Mrs Hollingsworth who was Bourne & Hollingsworth; there was the de Selingcourts, who were silk merchants; there were the Ailingworth's, who were cloth makers; there were the Royces, who were the biggest importers of champagne in those days. I can't remember any other ones, but they stick in my mind. There was a lot of money up at Hook Heath, there's a lot of money up there.

Before the War, we did have a van for delivery but not after the War. But I can remember – before the War of course this was – a telephone call coming from Chobham; one of our customers had lost his back stud and he was going out to a dinner. So what did I do, I went and got a back stud and took it out to him; it was worth a penny I think. I can remember that.
John Bailey

I decided I'd be going into an office, I mean there are far more openings these days. And I had sat two Civil Service exams and they took months before they even told you whether you'd passed, and I was getting a bit sort of fed up being at home where I couldn't see whether I'd passed or not, and my aunt sent me a cutting from the Daily Telegraph about the Legal and General were going to open a branch in Guildford and they wanted a shorthand typist, and so my aunt said, 'Perhaps you would like to apply for this,' so I wrote up and got the job.

We had to dress in either navy blue or something like that to go to the office in. When I first went to Legal and General, I first of all had to go up to their Head Office in Fleet Street, because they had to give me a bit of training. And as I say, there was this book and you had to sign in, and at 9.15 on the dot the red line was drawn; if you appeared below that three times in a month you were on the carpet! Very strict they were. And even the shorthand and typing requirements of the Legal and General were far, far higher than the Civil Service.
Joan Roberts

There was this book and you had to sign in, and at 9.15 on the dot the red line was drawn; if you appeared below that three times in a month you were on the carpet! Very strict they were.

Well, I went to Switzerland for a long summer to be a governess to a child whose father was the head of the hotel, the manager, and I lived with them and that was my start. My sister was still at school and after that, there was a vacancy at a little school in Woking. My mother said – she was always like a teacher, she was good that way – she said, 'Try teaching, maybe you'll find out at a little boys' prep school' – young sisters also went and that was the St Michael's School which is now Hoebridge School and that was that school and I was at its birth. I enjoyed being with the children – so that's what I did. I became a pupil teacher and got qualifications and taught various things.
Katharine Buchanan

Woking County School, 1930s. It was opened in 1914 as Woking County School for Boys and closed in July 1977. It is now Woking Police Station.
The Lightbox

Daily life on Chobham Road, Woking showing Wearing's the Chemist, Skeet and Jeffes and Meeks, the glass and china shop, 1930s *The Lightbox*

And so I started at Gammons and from the beginning I loved it. They gave me a broom and you had to go out to this back yard with a box and there was like sand, wet sand, and you had to shovel it into this thing, sprinkle it along the wooden floor and sweep it in front of you and that picked up the dust. Then you had to dust the chairs and set it all out, I mean, and you just did it. If you didn't do it properly, they'd say, you know, 'Oh you didn't sweep round there,' so you swept round there and have done with it.

Then eventually the window dresser wanted somebody to help him so I was selected and then you had to find the tickets and dust everything before you gave it to him and fetch what he wanted. We had two gentlemen, a window dresser and a gentleman in the outfitting and the remainder were all ladies, and the manager, and the others were all ladies.

And of course Miss Smith, she had a waist about eighteen inches round, no bigger, she was really old fashioned but she was a wonderful teacher. She was very patient and she would know if you'd been in her department to serve whilst she was at lunch, she would know whatever you'd touched, she'd know. But she taught you to be thorough, then of course, you were allowed to go behind the counter and you were the third person, you were allowed perhaps to sell a reel of cotton. And the first thing I was ever asked for and I hadn't a clue what it meant, the woman wanted buckram which you put in a waistband. Well, I didn't know what it was, and I crept up to the second girl and I said, 'This lady wants some buckleam.' But, whoever I worked with, they were always patient and that's what I made up my mind I would be if ever I got in charge.

We got to know the customers and

various things. And of course, all the ribbons were on paper, in rolls, all the cottons were in boxes, three of a colour and when you sold one, you had to go round to a little cupboard at the back and get another one and put it in. And if you sold out of anything as they called it, there was a book on the desk which you had to fetch and write it in. Woe betide you if you forgot that, if the manager came along to serve and you hadn't got it and it wasn't in the book. If it was in the book, you were out of danger.

And your books had to tally. You had to make a docket out even if it was only for a penny. Well of course, reels of Sylko were tuppence and, come stocktaking, everything had to be counted. I mean you counted the buttons in dozens and the ribbon all had to be undone and measured and then threaded back with the paper in between it and it had to be flat and then you put how much was on it, then come the time, the manager would come round to your department and if it was materials, you'd have a card in the side and it would say, and he would look through it and he'd ask you to find something then he would just check. And you didn't have a coffee break, or a tea break, only a tea break on Fridays and Saturdays. You weren't supposed to eat behind the counter but the apprentice would be sent up to Pullinger's to get six pennyworth of what was called wads, which were stale cakes, and you'd come back with a big bag of cakes which was surreptitiously put under the counter you see and nibbled. But of course that was all right until stock taking and then somebody would say, 'Don't forget, don't leave anything,' and one year, the manager was calling out and all of a sudden, he called out, 'One bag of buns.' He was a very good man, really. He was very strict, but he wasn't unjust.

And one day I got called to the office and, of course, you never called anybody by their Christian name, it was Miss Green, Mr Fooke, Miss Smith, you wouldn't dream – if he heard anybody he would say, 'This is not a social affair, this is a business house.' So you didn't do it. And he called me, he said, 'Your book is wrong, I don't agree the addition.' So I took it back, I mean, I wasn't bright at figures to start with, so I added it all up and I said, 'I'm sorry Mr Fooke, but I only find I'm a farthing out,' so he looked at me, he said, 'Well? Four farthings make a penny, twelve pennies make a shilling, twenty shillings make a pound, Miss.'

I enjoyed it though, and you met people and you got to know some people could be very nice, then you'd have the person who would come in and have the shop out, say, 'Well, I was only looking for my friend' and you began to know them. You knew if you fetched it all out she wouldn't buy anything. Then, of course, you had to fetch it out, it wasn't all laid out. Stockings and that were in boxes and you had to get the boxes down. And then men's caps, you had to go right through all the departments from ladies' fashions right through to the men's department and you sold men's overalls, shirts, flannelette shirts, cotton shirts, tunic shirts and then they were just going out then, men's stiff collars, because my father always wore a stiff collar.

Mind, you didn't shut the shop until the last customer had gone, so you were all hanging about if somebody was waiting, and you didn't dare put a dust cloth – you had to cover things over – you didn't dare start until the customer had gone.
Ada Green

With the running of the shop, we did get some of our supplies from Pratt's which was just on the railway line by the side of Victoria Arch. He used to have banana rooms as well, which was in Guildford Road, which you had to go and get your bananas from. They used to come over in great big ship loads and they used to be transported to the rooms for them to ripen off and then they were all boxed up, had great big long boxes and I was thinking so many pounds in a box and then this is how they used to bring them out to you.

When the War came along, things changed again because we had to ration everything and people was only allowed so much so therefore we couldn't get as much from the wholesalers so people used to queue up for odd things like bananas and other things and then I used to have to work with another piece of land which my father rented out down in Littlewick Road so that I was not called up, and that was the only way he could get me off, so I had to do that, manage the shop and look after the home and everything else on top of it. But we did manage, somehow or other.

My husband had some very good customers from The Hockering and Hook Heath and they always wanted certain things which he had to get in and they always wanted their cut flowers at Christmas time and also – oh, there was bulbs, there was the bulbs in the spring, the flowers in the spring which we grew at times. It did change quite a lot really until the super-markets come along and I'm afraid that was when we had to close up, really.
Irene Brice

I worked at Boots Library which was absolutely terrible. I hated it and I was still wearing ankle socks because I was only fifteen and I was really made fun of by the girls because they were all really smartly made up and I wasn't like that – I was very young for my age.

I worked at Boots Library. I was still wearing ankle socks because I was only fifteen.

Well, the Boots Library was frequented by the ladies. Most women didn't work then, middle class or even not so middle class; men did the work, women stayed at home and did all that work, a lot of work. But the ladies who came to Boots Library were more your middle class, Hook Heath type of people and they would go to Pullinger's for coffee, just across the road, coffee and cakes and with waitresses with white aprons and black frocks, and then they would come across to the library and what I had to do, as one of the library assistants, was to recommend books for them. Hardly any of them went down the shelves, pulled them out and had a look for themselves. They said things like, 'Well I want a nice romantic novel,' 'I want a family story' or 'I want this' and so, I would go down and I had to become quite aware of the books which I didn't mind, because I like books. I've always liked to read but in the end, I became a bit fed up with all this and I used to pull out the books and some-times just make up a story. I used to say, 'This is blah blah blah,' and 'That sounds in-teresting,' they'd say, and they'd take it off. I didn't get any complaints but that made life a bit more interesting.
Barbara Beaumont

They'd say things like, 'I want a nice romantic novel. I used to say, 'This is blah blah blah,' and 'That sounds interesting,' they'd say, and they'd take it off. I didn't get any complaints but that made life a bit more interesting.

My first job was as a lending librarian, which meant I was in charge of the lending library in Woking. I had several staff – mostly sort of young ladies – of varying ability really, some were better than others. I had one very fashionable young lady who always turned up in the latest sort of mini-skirts, hotpants, what-ever was the latest fashion. It was busy, it was quite fun really. And there was always quite a lot of work on advising readers on particular books they wanted, if they wanted particular fiction books, or books on topics. The Subscription Libraries had recently finished, and some elderly ladies who were still expecting to receive the service they had received from Boots or Smiths. You had staff running round, they couldn't just find the books they wanted. It was quite fun, and never a dull moment, you never knew what was going to hap-pen from one minute to the next, which was what I liked about it, you know, never a dull moment.
Rosemary Christophers

So Leslie Illingworth, I think my father approached him and got me a job in the Daily Mail in the photo library and they have thousands and thousands of pictures. Every picture that's taken comes in and goes in the library and the sort of thing that happens is that Leslie Illingworth would be drawing a cartoon with a telephone box in it and a Ford car and a lamppost and he'd say, 'Get me some pictures of a telephone box, a Ford car and a lamppost.' So I was there in the picture library for about three months and then they said there was a vacancy in the art room, would I like to go in there? Yes, I'd like to go in there, where I became an Assistant Night Art Editor.

Now this meant that you had photog-raphers in and you sent them out on jobs to cover jobs and you'd also get pictures in from news agencies, Associated Press, PA, Reuters, London News Agency, and then you would choose the best pictures, either of your own staff photographers or the news agency photographs – choose the ones, take them down to the editor and the editor would say, 'I'll have that one.' I'd make up all the pictures in the paper, take them in for retouching and chased it through, got them made into printing blocks, rushed them down to the printers downstairs, got the proofs of the photographs, took them up to the caption writers.
David Evans

Cycling to work at Florence House, Brookwood Hospital 1950s *The Lightbox*

I went to Brookwood very early on in 1990. It was an interesting place because I'd worked in a very similar hospital near Cambridge and some of the patients walking around seemed quite familiar though, of course, they weren't because they weren't people I knew at all. But there was a kind of run down feel to it when I went there. The first place I had to visit was the Occupational Therapy department. The OT departments are always sort of stuck out the back, round the back of hospitals. There was that sense that, you know, here they are, they're tacked on and there's the ad hoc feel to the buildings that are built and then there's this sort of contrast with the massive kind of Victorian solid corridors and big doors and all that sort of thing.

Well, I opted to work there and it was a practical reason because I had young children and I was sick of trying to hack my way through Guildford to get to Cranleigh. I went to meet the manager of the therapy services and she said, 'Well, there's work here at Brookwood if you can bear to work in a hospital again.' Because having worked in a community it's a bit of an unusual step to go back into hospital and I thought, 'Well, that would be OK actually.' I didn't mind. When you're in the community the responsibility is much greater because you tend to be the sole worker for a person with mental health problems, whereas when they're in a hospital you kind of share the involvement much more. So, in that sense, it's slightly less pressurised.
Wendy Bryant

I came back to Woking and stayed with my parents who were absolutely top of the pops and was in a bit of an emotional state and my mother said to me, 'You can't carry on like this, you've got to get a job, your mind is driving you crazy.' She said, 'I'll give up my part time job, I'll look after Jason,' who was my son. She said, 'You go out and sort yourself out.' And I just happened to look in the local paper and I saw a job for the Animal Virus Research Institute at Pirbright. So I phoned them up, went for an interview and they said, 'You're not supposed to come for an interview here, it's the Wellcome Laboratory next door,' and I said, 'Oh really.' So they said, 'Yes, you've got to go next door,' and it was exactly the time of the interview, so I had to leg it along to the next research laboratory and I was terribly nervous, and these three men were interviewing me in carpet slippers and really very casual and I was in a bit of a two-and-eight and the only thing they seemed to be concerned about was, was I going to go back to my ex-husband and I said, 'Certainly not, that's definitely not on the menu.' I couldn't say that I was thinking of going back to teaching, I thought I'd better keep it a bit cool. So I said, 'No, I'm thinking of a career and I've got to look after my son,' and all this kind of stuff and they said, 'We'll let you know' and the next day they rang me up and said, 'You've got the job.' So I started on a career in microbiology. I did that for a number of years and again, I think I had a personality transplant. I was sitting down one day and thinking, I really do like my job but I want to do something else. I want to do something that's more on a one-to-one basis, even though we were doing virus research and making vaccines for third world countries and things like this and for Europe. I thought, this is really good but I want to

do something else, and a friend of mine just happened to come into the canteen one day and he said, 'I'm thinking of doing a course in herbal medicine,' and I said, 'Are you, that sounds really exciting, tell me all about it.' So he went and sent away for all the details and I ended up leaving and doing the course.
Jennifer Wharam

They asked me where I would like to teach and I said, 'Well, in Woking, not too far from my home,' because public transport wasn't wonderful in those days, everybody rode bicycles, so you got on your bicycle, and I was rung up at the end of June by the Woking Education Office, and asked if I would like to start in Sheerwater, and could I start on the Monday morning because they were desperate for teachers. Now this was before September, so I'd only left college just the end of June, and I started in the August 1953.

Now in those days, Sheerwater was just being built. It was being built rapidly. It was an LCC – London County Council – estate and it was to house people who had lost their homes during the War and were in prefabs and all sorts of accommodation in London. Fullbrook School was being built, and so they used it for all the children that were coming into Sheerwater as the houses were occupied and they were desperate for teachers for the younger age range, so I went to Fullbrook. My father took me there on the Monday morning and the headmaster said to me 'You've got a class and there's fifty four in the class. I don't mind what you do, as long as you keep them quiet.' And there were fifty four five- and six-year-olds.
Barbara Chasemore

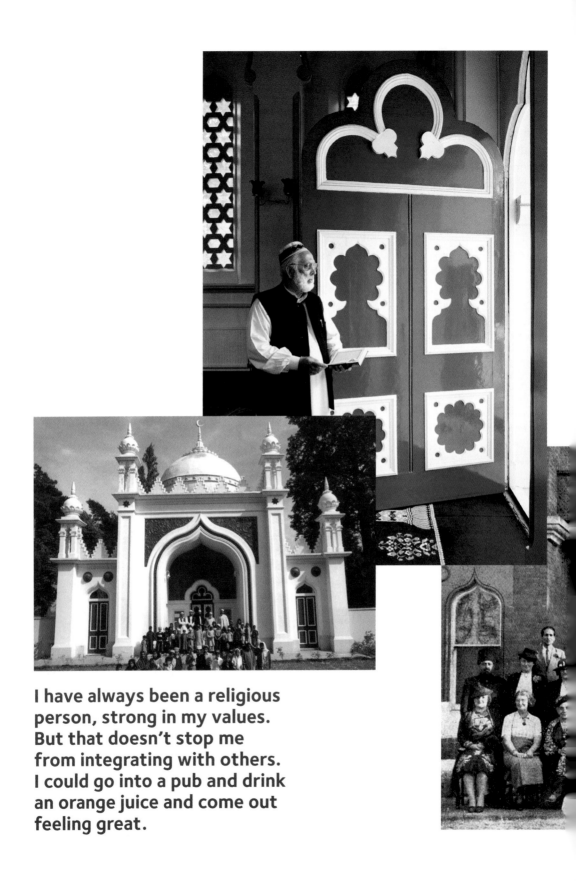

I have always been a religious
person, strong in my values.
But that doesn't stop me
from integrating with others.
I could go into a pub and drink
an orange juice and come out
feeling great.

The only thing that everybody wants is their sacred places to be respected by the other faith and religion.

There's always this consciousness of God being around and I think that's what really helped me along in that sense, stories of sacrifice and kindness and giving.

7. The Mosque and Islam

We are told that in the first ten years of the revival of the Mosque over a thousand British people were converted to Islam.

Drawing (unfortunately damaged) of Shah Jehan Mosque, 1889 *Serena Whiteman*

Well, I start off by telling you that the Mosque was built in 1889 and the name of the Mosque is the Shah Jehan Mosque; it is regarded as the first purpose-built mosque in the United Kingdom. There are other mosques at South Shields and Cardiff and Liverpool, which came otherwise, but in some cases they have not actually been purpose-built, just merely prayer halls.

Shah Jehan really is the name of the lady, and she was an Indian princess, and she was the ruler in her own right.

The name Shah Jehan of this mosque, is sometimes confused with the Mogul emperor Shah Jehan, the one who built the Taj Mahal in India. In this case Shah Jehan really is the name of the lady, and she was an Indian princess, and she was the ruler in her own right – not as the spouse of the ruler – of a small Indian state known as Bhopal. So that was the State in those days. So she is the person who gave the bulk of the money for the mosque to be built. It is reckoned at about £5,000.

Now, the project itself was of course not her idea. It was that of a German gentleman, his name was Dr Wilhelm Gottfried Leitner. He actually spent about twenty years in India from about 1865 to 1885 and while he was there he decided that he would like to start an Oriental Institute in Europe in fact. He could give degrees to people who are coming from the Indian subcontinent to study or work in the United Kingdom or in Europe, so that they could know something of how to live and the customs and the ways of life in the Western world; and in fact also to work in the other direction, for people who wanted to work in the Indian subcon-

tinent to know something of the culture and the languages in there. So it was to be that sort of Institute.

He was looking for a suitable site all over Europe and in fact it so happened that he was told that there was a Royal Dramatic College in Woking which was lying in a derelict condition. He bought this property for about £4,500 of his own money and started this Oriental Institute, which in some ways was a forerunner of the School of Oriental and African Languages in London. So it was a very far-sighted project.

As a matter of interest this Royal Dramatic College, as I said, was home for retired actors and actresses, and Charles Dickens was one of the governors of this institution.

The Mosque was in such a state that there was hay lying inside.

The Mosque was built under the guidance of a British architect, A.W. Chambers. He copied the style of the mosques that you find in the Indian subcontinent. It is in line with the fashion of the day, because here at that stage of development in the UK you have the Brighton Pavilion and all other buildings, some in London, which are fashioned after oriental institutions. After the death of Dr Leitner the Mosque went into more or less disuse, except on occasional times, until about 1912, when an Indian lawyer whose name was Mr Kamal-ud-Din came to try and propagate Islam in England. He came and he started his work in Kingston, and was somehow told about the Woking Mosque, and he came over and he actually sort of fell in love with the site. In fact I'm told that at that stage, the Mosque was in such a state that there was

Kamal-ud-Din and his successors did a lot of work in propagating Islam, and we are told that in the first ten years of the revival of the Mosque – say up to about 1930 or so – over a thousand British people were converted to Islam.

Children at Mela festival, 1997 *Salma Sulaimani*

Hazrat Khwaja Kamal-ud-Din with English new converts (left to right) Omar Wilkins, Fatima Wilkins and Osman Watkins, 1926 *www.wokingmuslim.org*

hay lying inside, and maybe even some cattle were tethered inside, but I am not very sure about that. But he came, he cleaned up the place and re-established the Mosque as a regular praying constituent. And ever since then the Mosque has been in use, at least five times a day, if not more.

Kamal-ud-Din and his successors did a lot of work in propagating Islam, and we are told that in the first ten years of the revival of the Mosque – say up to about 1930 or so – over a thousand British people were converted to Islam, and the work carried on.

Now one of the most essential parts other than prayer that the Mosque is responsible for is the religious education of our younger children, growing up. And so the Mosque has been running a school, a religious school every weekday for many, many years. It is being run every day, from say about half-past four to half-past six. And they are taught there a few things. The first one they are taught is the Muslim prayer; if their parents have already not done so, they are taught that. Then they are taught how to read Arabic, because the Koran, our holy book, is in Arabic, so how to read it. Then they are also taught something about the life of our Prophet, the Prophet Mohammed, Peace Be Upon Him, and also something of the history of Islam, and the customs and requirements of a good Muslim. Over the years we have found that progress at the school has not been very good, particularly because some of the teachers, or the Imams that we have, they are all from Pakistan. And most of them perhaps are coming from the religious schools, and their method of teaching is as perhaps for a thousand years ago. So in the modern age the modern systems have not been used, and we found that the output was not as good as we would like.

So in our search we have now found a person who is actually from South Africa. He's a Muslim from South Africa, perhaps of Indian or Pakistani origin, but has been brought up and so is a little better acquainted with the methods of teaching. In fact, since he has been here for a year now[5], a little over a year, our school which used to have about a hundred and twenty, a hundred and thirty children, has now shot up to over three hundred children.
Brigadier Muslim Salamat

Well then the Mosque came along and of course it was a great mystery and they didn't come much into the town but everybody was a little bit nervous, but I don't think there was any discrimination. I think they just kept themselves to themselves. There was – now I've forgotten the people's name at the moment – there was an antique shop at the top of Walton Road and I think one of the young ladies there got to know one of these gentlemen. Some people would say, 'You know she could be one of many wives.' I mean that was all hearsay! And then eventually you could go into the Mosque and they would show you round. I went once. It was very pleasant and they were very quiet and nobody ever took any notice.
Ada Green

5 In early 2004. (Ed.)

Wedding Reception of Mr Salah-ud-din Ahmed Toto and Miss Olive Zeytoun Howell, 1939
www.wokingmuslim.org

First party on leave from the Indian contingent of the British Expeditionary Force, to say Jum'a prayers on 10th May 1940. Major J.W.B Farmer, a Woking convert to Islam, is seated in the third row, second from the left. *www.wokingmuslim.org*

And I do remember during the War, seeing – before Partition of course in India – the Indian soldiers coming off the trains looking extremely smart in their uniforms, lining up outside the station and marching down Oriental Road to the Mosque for particular feast days; because there were very few mosques around at that time.
Bernadette Rivett

Major Farmer and his daughter Elizabeth reading the Qu'ran at Woking Mosque, 1959 *Elizabeth Farmer*

In Sheerwater at that time there were very few Asian children and then I made friends with one English girl. I still remember her to this day. And she left after a year in fact. I made friends with her, I don't know how we communicated but we did. And she used to help me in the class. And then, after that, we didn't have any support in education. There wasn't any extra lessons or bilingual staff or anything. No help at all. In fact, I remember the first day I went to that school and I wore my – it was a uniform. Grey skirt and white blouse and blue cardigan and I wore my trousers underneath and my scarf. The first day I went to the school and the teacher there told me to take everything off. Had to take my trousers off because it wasn't allowed. It was very upsetting obviously but, as a child, I didn't really know what to expect, you know? But it was very upsetting because then I was twelve-and-a-half, thirteen, very shy, very embarrassed, you know? A typical twelve - , thirteen-year-old really. I didn't really get much support from my mum because of the language. I used to wear my trousers to school, take them off in school, wear them at home time and walk back.
Nighat Jobeen

There's always this consciousness of God being around and that's really helped me along, stories of sacrifice, kindness and giving.

He says, 'Ee, you speak perfect English, why don't you help those Pakistani ladies who come to me and I can't understand them, to diagnose?'

One good incident, or funny incident, which I can certainly relate to you: being the month of Ramadan now, in those days it used to be also in winter. So people used to get up early in the morning and they would go visiting each others' houses at four o'clock in the morning and the police started arresting them, not realising what they are doing, okay? Now that was the period when my wife and I slowly and gradually started participating in the local life, if I can use that word, in the sense that my wife started interpretation for one of the doctors' surgeries. The doctor's surgery used to be on York Road, a Scottish doctor. We joined him and when he spoke to my wife, he says, 'Ee, you speak perfect English, why don't you help those Pakistani ladies who come to me and I can't understand them, to diagnose?' So she said, 'Yes, okay I will help, no problem at all. If you have a patient I will come round.' So slowly and gradually we then started getting involved.

We formed a little association known as the Pakistani Cultural Group. And police were actually looking for somebody from the community with whom they could liaise and understand what were the reasons. So when these guys got arrested, Mr Zahir went to the police station and said, 'Why have you arrested them?' They said, 'Well, they are roaming around on the road, they are roaming around on the road at four o'clock in the morning,' you know, so he has to explain to them. Once that explaining was done, police then understood it and then, you know, we slowly and gradually got involved with the police and if there was a person arrested and there was a need for an interpreter my wife would go or I would go or Mr Zahir would go and help them, you know, with the interview application and so on and so forth.

You see, there was an association, and has always been. There are two associations related to masses of Pakistanis, one is known as Pakistani Welfare Association, the other is known as Kashmir Welfare Association. The main purpose of both of those associations in those days was that anybody who died, their relations wanted their bodies to be sent to Pakistan and because there were not sufficient financial resources available with the individual to be sent back, they said, 'Well we'll form an Association, you will pay £4/£5 a year or £10 a year and if any person dies and his relatives want the body to be sent to Pakistan, we'll do that.'
Dr A Mahoon

Members of the Muslim community outside the Shah Jehan Mosque
Surrey History Centre

My father always used to tell us stories of the old prophets and things like that. I think when you are younger, you just do take it in. You might not remember it up here in the head, but you do kind of have that inclination builds up. There's always this consciousness of God being around and I think that's what really helped me along in that sense, stories of sacrifice and kindness and giving.

Obviously there's the Prophet Mohammed, Peace Be Upon Him, he's obviously very important for us, and even Jesus, Isa in Islam, how he used to cure the blind and always used to be kind and tell stories. He used to tell stories like that. My father tried to teach me Urdu and, even in the Urdu books, there's all stories about how different people, even if it was just a story about an old lady, for instance, she was a Muslim and she did this and this. I think they just

kind of sunk in somewhere. Must have done. But there wasn't this like nowadays, when people just send their children to the Mosque to learn Arabic. We learnt it at home. I still haven't got the right pronunciation because my parents did the best they knew how. Also we used to go to this other lady to learn as well. But there wasn't this Mosque, there wasn't that kind of influence or anything like that.

At school I was into music. Always into music and fashion. Pop music. What was in the charts then and everything. Things like that, anything that's number one. I don't think I ever bought an album or anything like that. My parents weren't too keen on me listening to music. The only way I got a tape recorder was my brother-in-law was trying to get rid of one and I took it.
Interviewee

Out of school it was very routine.
I used to come home and go to the Mosque, come back from Mosque, do my homework, have my dinner, go to bed.

I can only speak about myself. I haven't experienced racism although I am a working parent. My children go to local schools and, then again, it's all about communicating I think. If you can communicate with somebody and they can understand where you're coming from... I mean, I would never go out in trousers and a top just to please somebody. I'm very proud of who I am and I would never change my dress sense just to fit in with somebody. But I think it's lack of understanding, again, and lack of... If people don't know, they will be frightened and that's where problems start I think. If they don't know the language, the culture, the dress they're suddenly, 'Oh, my God! That's a strange person here.' And I think that's where problems start.
Nighat Jobeen

Well, I'm afraid I'm biased. I've always maintained, throughout my life, always, that I'm not racist. And I'm not. I honestly am not because I think everybody is born the same, we all die the same and we're entitled to live a decent life. But Maybury estate has been earmarked for Pakistanis, Asians. And my grandson was very, very ill over ten, twelve years ago. He got very severe kidney trouble and I wanted my daughter near me and she went to Woking Council and asked if she could come on to the Maybury estate if ever a house became vacant. And she was told, categorically, that any houses that became vacant on Maybury were earmarked for Asians. And when we challenged it afterwards they denied they said it but I am, here and now, stating that that was said, in my presence and my daughter's.

> **It's wrong, especially against children. Children all over the world are exactly the same. I don't care if they're black, pink, yellow or whatever colour. They're children and they've a right to be respected.**

But, you know, I mean I've got next door neighbours now that are Asian, Pakistani, and they are lovely people. They really are lovely people and if I wanted anything done they'd jump, you know? Christmas time, I asked if – because they both run taxis, both the husbands next door – they took my husband and I all the way over to Chobham and came and picked us up and wouldn't accept a penny. But what does get me where they're concerned is, it's no good saying that they integrate because they don't. They do not. I mean, I've got a neighbour along here I've known for donkey's years. They say, 'Hello.' They're polite but there's no friendliness, you know? Like in the old days we all knew one another's business. Nosiness, what you like, we always knew what was going on in one another's homes. There's nothing like that now. They've had to put up with a lot of abuse. I know that because I've heard it myself and I've gone out there and I've put a stop to it because I don't believe in it. It's wrong, especially against children. Children all over the world are exactly the same. I don't care if they're black, pink, yellow or whatever colour. They're children and they've a right to be respected. We all have a right to be respected.
Pamela Peachey

We are living in a capsule, the people of Woking, Manchester, Glasgow, whatever – they've moved on but we're still living in that time span where they came from, because when they go back home, they find 'God, they've moved on' – we're still living in their parents' time when they came here.

It wasn't too bad actually in school. I mean there was the odd occasion where people regard you as being a Paki or whatever. I always thought that it was only people who had nothing else to say would say it because they had nothing else to attack. Or if they weren't happy with something they would just say it to you. On the other hand I did get people who would say to me, 'I'm not saying it to you. I'm saying it to them.' And I said, 'Well, I am them for God's sake.' And I remember, at work, I used to get this lady say, 'Oh, all of them smell.' And all this … 'I'm not saying it to you.' And I said, 'For God's sake it could be my mother you could be talking about and I know she…' It's just a generalisation. You've seen one person who's like that and then you think that everybody's all the same and I couldn't understand that. I said, 'You shouldn't … basically you should say it in front of me.' Either I am going to be the same as them or … I can't just pretend I'm not Pakistani. My parents are Pakistani, we're all … our origins are there.
Interviewee

But I think it's lack of understanding. If people don't know, they will be frightened and that's where problems start I think

We are living in a capsule, the people of Woking, Manchester, Glasgow, whatever – they've moved on but we're still living in that time span where they came from, because when they go back home, they find 'God, they've moved on' – we're still living in their parents' time when they came here. So this is a bit of a thing, they are now slowly and steadily realising, the parents are realising, and now hopefully things will become better for the children. The reason is because that's the upbringing they've had, so they are forcing that on their children. Because Islam says go on the straight path, that's all what it says, keep the word and keep your religion – intermingle the two, don't be an extremist and this is what people have to learn. Because you see the Koran, people have not read the Koran, because it's written in Arabic, so we don't know the meaning, we just do it by reading it. Because in the villages, what happens is the Imam's there – anybody can say what they like because nobody's checking them, so they have got onto their own sort of religion. It's not what the Koran says or the books that were written about the Holy Prophet from other sources. They're not listening to that, they're giving their own interpretation of things and just to suit them.
Rafeea Mahoon

Islam says if you want to mingle with men, it's for your own good that you cover your head, because hair is a thing of beauty so you should cover your hair and don't attract the opposite sex. That's the only thing behind it.

We have a very strict way of life. Because we are being Muslims, everything revolves around the Holy Koran and we are bound by that. Everything's laid out for us and we just follow it automatically. So when the teachers at school would say, this child is not learning and I'd say that's not possible. This child goes to the Mosque and he reads the Holy Koran and you have to have something up there to learn the Koran. You think, he can learn the Koran and memorise passages, he can't be thick, there's something that is not getting him to do the proper thing, to learn. So he's not daft, so there should be another way of handling it or looking into it.

I was asked if I could be the governor of Park School, that's the school for disabled, for children with learning disabilities, and I was the governor there for sixteen years. It was just guiding the teachers and the head as to if a problem comes in, why is this problem there? They have to understand this child is not ...... because at home, he's got a different way of life. When he comes to school or she comes to school, she has to behave in a very different way. Back home, they don't have dining tables to sit on you see because in the Muslim world, you segregate the men and the women. So the men and the boys are given food before the ladies and the girls

would have food, and then in the dining room, they would all sit together – that was confusing for those children. There's so many things. Back home, we always eat with our hands – the right hand – and here they were using knives and forks. So in the normal schools as well, there's a lot of other things that happen, that people do not understand why is the child behaving that way. There's a lot of change for them to get accustomed to but God willing – and I thank God for that – they've done very well and I'm very proud to say that now the children have grown up, they've got married and they've got children.

There are some parents that they require the girls to wear the hijab, well that's in Islam. Islam says if you want to mingle with men, it's for your own good that you cover your head, because hair is a thing of beauty so you should cover your hair and don't attract the opposite sex, you're fine. That's the only thing behind it – nothing more, nothing less.

Now I think the parents say that there's no point bringing a boy from Pakistan or a girl from Pakistan, because the mental attitudes are very different. So now they're looking and they're encouraging their children to find somebody in this country.

Usually the Mosque is the men's domain because men congregate for prayers five times a day. So women are supposed to be... if they've got nothing to do, they can go to the Mosque but usually women stay at home because they've got children to look after and their duties in the house. So that's the reason why they don't go, but on Friday because it's like your Sunday Mosque, people go there on a Friday and you meet a few women. Really on Fridays, it's about two thousand people.
Rafeea Mahoon

My mum said, 'You can get married whenever you like.' My dad doesn't really care. I would marry a Muslim. I don't care if he's Malaysian, Arabian – just Muslim.

It's quite a big population and most of the male members have come in the '50s and '60s and they are established here and then they have brought their families later on and so most of them have come in to their own culture as it were and they have settled down and not made an effort to change because they think it's too late or they can't do it. I don't think there is a culture shock for them. It is culture shock seeing the surroundings but, you know, they are not bothered about that, I think. They've got their own world. That's what I think – their food, their clothes, their religion, everything. They are retaining that. Which is not a bad thing. I mean, they are free to do what they feel like and nobody would want them to change their clothes or their food or their religious belief. But the children and the language, the children are changing. They wear western clothes. They eat western foods, McDonald's... They speak English, they have the education and they are keeping to their tradition also, to some extent, which is very good. Their marriage system is still that they have arranged marriages in the sense that the parents suggest and they marry in the family and all that. They keep to their religion. It's just a good thing.
Mumtaz Ashraf

When you get used to it, when you grow up with it you like fit in nicely. It's okay, it's not all that bad.

I find some images offensive but then they're not that bad, as everyone says they is. Like everyone says, 'Oh, my God. They're so bad.' But it isn't. When you get used to it, when you grow up with it you like fit in nicely. It's okay, it's not all that bad.

My parents take it that if the girl covers herself it looks better. Because my parents, they say that, 'Look, showing your body off doesn't give you a big name or something.' It's not my parents that have got something wrong with it, it's just that other people, they talk and they say, 'Oh, my God. We saw this person's daughter doing this.'
Young person

Well my mum got married when she was like eighteen and she was innocent, just about. She didn't really know about marriage and that lot and she goes, 'You can do whatever you like. You can get married whenever you like.' And there's actually arranged marriages and she got an arranged marriage and she goes that she didn't like it. It's not that she didn't like her husband, my dad, but she didn't know my dad that well and she was scared and that. She said, 'You can get married whenever you like.' My dad doesn't really care.

I would marry a Muslim. I don't care if he's Malaysian, Arabian – just Muslim.
Student

Interior of the doorway at the Mosque, with Mabboob Hussain, 2002
English Heritage. NMR

Interior of the Shah Jehan Mosque, 2002 *English Heritage. NMR*

> **The only thing that everybody wants is their sacred places to be respected by the other faith and religion.**

Now we are in a very strange position. I personally don't know what's the solution of it. Because the children, those who are born here, brought up here, it is very difficult for them to get accepted there, because it's entirely two different cultures and those children who are having the language problem they feel more comfortable speaking English rather than their own languages because they are born here, brought up here. Their friends and everything. It's not easy for them to get settled back home.

The older people there are a little bit... because, as I told you that I was working in an ethnic minority advice centre and when I was working there I notice that there are conflicts within the families because the older people, they expect from the children the behaviour, the attitudes, the lifestyle as they were living back home. But these children, they haven't seen these things. They are not aware of their culture, tradition and other things. So it's difficult to adopt these things over here. But, now the older people are becoming a little bit flexible or trying to understand the reasons. What are the reasons? But still there are some people who wants that the children should go back, get settled there.

There are family traditions, there are other things, especially in Islamic countries. People prefer that their girls and daughters that they should marry in a proper way. Like this sort of open friendship are going here and there it's not liked in these countries because of their culture. But if a boy or a son do something wrong perhaps the parents they can absorb that. They can accept that. If girls do the same thing it's more hurting for the parents.

> **The older people, they expect from the children the behaviour, attitudes, and lifestyle as they were living back home. But these children haven't seen these things. They are not aware of their culture, tradition and other things. So it's difficult to adopt these things over here.**

The only source of the Mosque is the income we generate on the Friday, when people come for Friday prayer, whatever they can afford. £1, £2, £5, £10, whatever they can easily afford. They donate to the Mosque and you would be pleased to know that, in the last ten, twenty years, we have spent nearly half a million pounds. And now we have got three big halls where, at a time, about twenty-seven, twenty-eight hundred people can say their prayers, especially on real occasions, we get round about two thousand people. Between two and three thousand people from the surrounding towns and, sometimes, people come from London because this was the oldest Mosque and people still have their attachment with this and that's why they come over here.

Ghazala Waheed with young people at the Maybury Centre *Ghazala Waheed*

I am the local trustee for the Mosque and with the previous Imam we tried to organise the inter-faith dialogue. That exercise went very well. There were round about two to three hundred people from the white community. They visited. First time they came to the Mosque and everybody was saying to me that we are living in Woking for the last twenty years but this is first time we are visiting the Mosque. Because we feel that the Mosque is for everybody. Now, whoever wants to come into the Mosque for their prayer we don't mind. Either they're Muslim, Christian or whatever, they can pray in the way they like. But the only thing that everybody wants is their sacred places to be respected by the other faith and religion.

Five years back we had the first function and we invited the Priest, the Reverend. It was the open invitation for everybody and people were really happy. The first time they noticed that the attitude of the people are very welcoming. The food was served, free of charge and the people liked the food as well. And when we noticed that it is going well, then the second programme was organised in the church, just opposite the mosque, in Oriental Road and they invited the Muslim community over there and we went there. We were quite happy to, because these things bring us close and it helps to understand each other in a better way.
Mohammad Ilyas Raja

I remember having a phone call from a woman who said, 'Oh, you were out in the town today?' I said, 'I didn't see you.' 'No, actually so and so saw so and so, who said, "So and so saw you and you were out."' There was this constant watchful eye.

I felt suffocated, really felt suffocated. I remember for the first two months I was so unsettled I kept saying to my husband, 'Can we not leave, can we not go back?' I remember being out shopping and having come home and having had a phone call from a woman who said, 'Oh, you were out in the town today?' I said, 'I didn't see you.' 'No, actually so and so saw so and so, who said, "So and so saw you and you were out."' There was this constant sort of watchful eye and then I also remember going along to a meeting, with my husband, at the community centre and being told off by one of the ladies afterwards, 'You know, wives don't do these things. We don't really appreciate you doing these things. Going and sitting with men.' It wouldn't stop me. They found it strange that I could drive. Imam's wife driving a car. It hadn't happened, I think there. All along they'd had very traditional, elder individuals as Imams and, obviously, the older Imams' wives who observed purdah to the max, weren't visible. That's what the communities were used to, so to have an Imam's wife who was out working, mixing, driving a car and all that!

My husband and I worked alongside each other. He was the Imam but he and I worked together in the Mosque for five years, very closely. We brought about a lot of change. Good change I would say. When we moved into Woking women seldom came to the Mosque, purely it was an all man's patch. That's where they gathered around and have a natter and a gossip about the community. It was theirs, you know? It was their space, even though it's a public arena. It wasn't meant to be for women. You know, whatever you want to do you do at home, in terms of worship, prayer, etc. No place for you in the Mosque. They weren't welcomed.

We moved into Woking 22nd August 1996. That very same week I started classes, basic Islamic study classes, open to everybody of all ages, including women. Mine were all girls' classes and I had, at that time, on my register, I remember, eighty to a hundred and twenty women, young girls. Of all ages. There was, obviously, a desire to learn. People wanted to, young women wanted to, they wanted to go to the Mosque and then, obviously, things progressed. To the disliking of some. Because it wasn't in their vested interests to see things moving in that way. They were almost sort of losing control of this space that was theirs. And, also, we opened the Mosque up to the wider community.

But the Pakistani community in Woking is very male chauvinistic. Women are expected to be seen and not heard.

Ladies at a Ham Nawa ('like-minded people') function where music and poetry is enjoyed *Surrey History Centre*

In effect, there's a lot of lip service that is paid to the fact that these people are very religious and they're practising, but often what they practise is not a religion. Not the Islamic religion, not the Muslim religion. What they practice is a culture and the culture is that of South Asia. There's a lot of confusion over exactly what they do. I mean, there's obviously a generation issue but also a cultural issue as well.

The differences are Islam permits women, a woman, a girl to receive an equal education as that of her male counterpart bearing in mind that she is properly covered and that she is leading her life in accordance to the Koran and the sayings of the prophets. The Koran doesn't say, 'Send your girls to school up until they're sixteen and then sit them at home and get them married off and don't let them do anything else. Whereas you can let your boys run riot. Come in at five o'clock in the morning, no questions asked and your girl is not allowed out of the house.'

Okay, people might not agree to some of things that I do or some of things that I say, but I'm justified as long as I know that what I'm doing is in accordance to the Islamic tradition, I don't have a problem as long as my husband feels that what I'm doing is right. I'm answerable to God, not to the Woking community. But the Pakistani community in Woking is very male chauvinistic. Women are expected to be seen and not heard. Many of the men who you will see appearing at different levels across the community, in terms of 'as community representatives' are usually self-elected, are usually there because of who they know and how much strength their particular grouping has within the community. These men will... you never see their wives.

Salma Sulaimani

If you've got anti-social behaviour and the person is young there's a process of education, we ask the Mosque to educate them.

The first time I went to the Mosque was probably when I was seven, eight. I think I was reading the Koran and learning. It was like a school there. After school, 4.30 to 5.30. I used to go there to learn. You know, Islam and stuff.
School student

Firstly, we were unfamiliar with the culture of complaint. And then there was also a problem with language. So we tended to avoid complaining and often fought our own battles.

If you've got anti-social behaviour and the person is young, where the police have got limited power, we go to the Mosque and ask them. First we go the parents and ask them, 'Is this a problem?' And they deal with it, the parents. And then, if they think the same problem is there, there's a process of education, we ask the Mosque to educate them. And that way we handle it and did a good job.
Sultan Khan

Mayor Ian Fidler listens to a speaker outside the Shah Jehan Mosque at the Mela festival, c.2000 *Surrey History Centre*

We had this unfortunate era at that time of 'Paki bashing' and I wouldn't say racial hatred – racial maybe in a different sense. But ignorance, I put it down to. At that time we were a little scared of going to school in the morning, but once we were there we felt assured, yes, possibly okay. But the second part came when we were leaving school, because we had to walk to and from school and we would often get picked on at the school gates, picked on by older boys, older white boys. The scenario was to do a 'Paki bashing.'

When I look back at it now and think about these things, I feel that we were not best served by the teaching staff at the time. Firstly, we were unfamiliar with the culture of complaint, which was that we came from a part of the world whereby you don't complain to teachers, you deal with it yourself. And then there was also the barrier of complaining, because we had a problem with language. So we tended to avoid complaining and often fought our own battles. The police was involved in one or two instances because there was a difference of fighting as well. The white children were good at boxing and kicking, whereas the Pakistani children, we tend to be – out of frustration probably – tend to fight with objects more than anything else. No knives, we wouldn't go to that extent, but we would often hide bike pumps or things that we could possibly use to defend ourselves and, if need be, we used them. I remember one or two fights that turned pretty violent and that was the time that possibly the school and the police got involved because they realised that things were getting out of control.

I have always been a religious person, religious and strong in my values, strong in my approach. But that doesn't stop me from integrating with others at the same level. I could go into a pub and drink an orange juice and come out feeling great.

The majority of the Pakistanis that have arrived here in Woking are from Pakistan, from the Punjab and from Mirpur and that area of Kashmir. There are also some from other Muslim countries, like Bangladesh, like we have now some from other parts of Pakistan as well. But at the same time, the majority of the Islamic world is Sunni. There is not a big problem on that at all, it's just that we all have our likes and dislikes, we all have our practices.

I have always been a religious person, religious and strong in my values, strong in my approach. But that doesn't stop me from integrating with others at the same level. I could go into a pub and drink an orange juice and come out feeling great. I didn't need to hold a glass of beer just to be acceptable, so that's how strong I am and that's how strong, hopefully, 'insh'Allah' I will remain.
Shamas Tabrez

There was always a main feature film and then there was a second film and then there was usually a cartoon and loads of adverts. Of course, we had the news as well. It was a good programme for 1/6d wasn't it?

We had tennis parties and gatherings. The hostesses wore hats indoors, little straw hats maybe in the summer – imagine! – and the visitors came with gloves and hats.

8. Sport and Leisure

The only training regime with the Woking Rovers was that you had to go and put the goal post up and the nets etc. and you didn't actually do any training, you just turned up.

There was no nonsense, there was no hanky panky, it never even crossed my mind because we just didn't behave like that.

Swifts Tennis Club tea party, 1938 *Ann Squibb*

We had tennis parties and gatherings, but always a special 'Big Tea' – which was necessary because dinner was served around eight o'clock (whereas North America had theirs around five-six o'clock). The ladies – the hostesses – wore hats indoors, little straw hats maybe in the summer – imagine! – and the visitors came with gloves and hats. This was in a private house and the hostess wore a hat. It was extraordinary – it was so Victorian, left over, this etiquette business.

We all wore whites to play tennis. Oh yes, very much so. We were just beginners and had coaching in the holidays and went to each other's places.

At the tea parties you always had bread and butter first – nice bread, sometimes homemade – but that was the start and then you had something hot, sometimes buns or scones. Then you had sandwiches and a buttered bread or a sticky fruit loaf and then two cakes, one of which was usually fruit and the other something else. These routines we loved. It was just something that was different and more casual. *Katherine Buchanan*

We had tennis parties and gatherings. The hostesses wore hats indoors, little straw hats maybe in the summer – imagine! – and the visitors came with gloves and hats.

Racing cars at the ready at Brooklands, 1938 *Ann Squibb*

We used to swim in the canal in the summer as children. It was filthy. You'd see the odd dead dog floating in it. We swam in it – it didn't seem to affect us. We never caught any disease or anything like that. All the kids did.
Sir Alec and Eric Bedser

We used to swim in the canal in the summer as children. It was filthy. You'd see the odd dead dog floating in it.

We had plenty of countryside and, when I first started school they were racing on the Brooklands Track, the motor racing, and I can remember that quite plainly, coming out of school and going and watching the motor racing on the track, so there was always something going on in this area.
Geoffrey Simpson

Officials at Woking FC for Whit Monday Sports, early 1920s *Ann Squibb*

They had sports days at Woking, where they've got the football pitch now. The police used to hold a sports day on the Whitsun Monday and the railway used to hold it on the August Bank Holiday Monday, but it could be the opposite of what I'm telling you; but they used to run it and they used to have athletics. They had a funfair there, cycling events and tug of war events so that all the people in the area went to it. I can remember to this day we used to take part and when we came back – my mother and father and brother and sister and friends – we used to have a salad tea with salmon and jelly and ice cream and cake and we really looked forward to that. It was great, they were great days.
Fred Woodhouse

Then sports days was the sack race, the egg and spoon race – they're all the same now really aren't they? – the flowerpot race and the slow bicycle race, which they do today don't they? Quite good fun.

Later we did tennis, we did hockey, we did netball, and sport was always included in the day and gym – everybody did it. We were very active. It wasn't like extra after school, it was part of the day, everybody always did the gym and the games for an hour a day. You had to, unless you'd broken a leg or something – there was no excuse.
Wendy Davenport

Yes, yes, we had good fun during the summer playing cricket. We could play quite happily in the street because there was so little traffic.

Yes, yes, we had good fun during the summer playing cricket. We could play quite happily in the street because there was so little traffic; or in Brewery Road, now a car park, there was a lovely playing field adjacent to the canal and we could play cricket all day long if we wished. If you hit the ball into the canal that was six and you were out, and we did get a team together now and again. There was a very kind lady in Woodham Road, Horsell, Mrs Hanning and she would arrange now and again a cricket match on the Horsell Cricket Ground just by the oak tree on the end of Brewery Road, beginning of Church Hill. The great highlight of the afternoon was the break for tea, when we all rushed into the pavilion and Mrs Hanning provided sandwiches, cakes and lemonade which was really a treat for us all.
William Ledger

In the school holidays we would mostly play in the woods or go to Woking swimming pool. We used to walk everywhere. Walked to Woking swimming pool for swimming or play over the canal. Doing silly things.
Barry Pope

We used to have a salad tea with salmon and jelly and ice cream and cake and we really looked forward to that. It was great, they were great days.

My father, William Victor Clewley, was quite a well-known figure locally because he participated in various events with the Woking Electric Supply Company's concert party, which was very active in the 1930s. He was a song and dance man.

I attended the class of 1935 in the Horsell Church of England School on the hill. Miss Field was my teacher and she was very strict. She was very keen on the boys doing Morris dancing and she took us for country dancing. She used to compete in the various schools, showing the boys off in their Morris dancing. I still remember 'The Flowers of Edinburgh' and things like that.
Pamela Green

We used to all go down to what they call The Patch, which has got houses on now, and we used to play football down there most days. We didn't really have a very good football but we used to play on The Patch.
Philip Ledger

My teacher was very keen on the boys doing Morris dancing. She used to compete in the various schools, showing the boys off in their Morris dancing.

Alec Bedser bowling for England in a test trial and his twin brother Eric Bedser batting for The Rest. Eric scored 30 runs for The Rest, some of them off his brother's bowling, 1951 *EMPICS/PA*

No lessons, never had a lesson in our life. We became good at cricket because that was our sole interest really, and from the age of six or seven, somehow we became mad on it.

We had no playing fields – played on a bit of dirt. We had organised football, but there was no real organised cricket at all, except two matches a year for the school and no proper pitches to play on. We played on dirt.

No lessons, never had a lesson in our life. We became good at cricket because that was our sole interest really, and from the age of six or seven, somehow we became mad on it. We played when we could amongst ourselves and also amongst the choir. We used to run a choir team – we were in the church just across there from where we are now, in Anthony's, and from the age of about seven or eight we used to all get together, get two sides and play.

We had one bat between the team. We had some old stumps, or it didn't matter, there were plenty of trees. You used to use a tree as a stump. You don't need a lot of equipment to learn how to play cricket. All you need is a bat and a ball and if you're keen enough, you'll get out and find a way of doing it.

We only started to play for Woking when we were about fifteen or sixteen, so we'd already started work then. So we didn't play much cricket at all – not organised cricket – when we were boys; we played, as we said, amongst ourselves, but not in any real organised team. There was no youth cricket or anything like that, like there is today. All there was, was a local club side, which we joined when we were about fifteen or sixteen and played in their second XI for a year I suppose, and then we went up and played in the first team until we were nineteen. This was unpaid. You had to pay a sub to play. The sub was a guinea a year to play for the club. It was more than a week's wages.

We were so mad on playing and when we got to about age eighteen, we made up our minds virtually that we wanted to play cricket. By that time, we'd become good enough for the county to be interested. We were fortunate that an ex-salaried professional ran a little cricket school at Woking and he was then appointed coach at the Oval and he must have thought we had potential, so he recommended us for a trial at the Oval. It was just sheer luck really – haphazard – and we went and played in the trial and did all right, and so they offered us a contract.

We had one bat between the team. We had some old stumps, or you used to use a tree as a stump. You don't need a lot of equipment to learn how to play cricket. All you need is a bat and a ball and if you're keen enough, you'll get out and find a way of doing it.

I doubt whether we would have gone in for cricket as a profession, but when I was running – or supporting – a department, there was a senior clerk and I was a junior and I used to look after it when he was away, and when I reached the age of about eighteen-and-a-half or nineteen I was running this department when he was away. But then a fellow joined the firm who was a public schoolboy and he joined

and I found that he was being paid twenty-five shillings a week or thirty shillings a week and I was getting eighteen. So I went to the partner and said, 'Why is it he's getting all this more and yet I'm showing him what to do?' He said, 'Well he went to a public school and you didn't.' So we said, 'Well if that's the case, we'll go somewhere where that doesn't matter.' That's how we went.

To enlarge on that, what we said was, we'd go somewhere that, if we do well, we get paid for it. But it was a hell of a risk to become a professional. It was only a yearly contract, that's all – year to year – never any more. If you weren't any good, you got the sack.
Sir Alec and Eric Bedser

There was Jack Francis who ran a coal yard and he had his horses out in one of the fields in South Road with the cows and he was a keen Oddfellow. So the Oddfellows started a cricket team and Jack said, 'Well if you can make anything of it, you're welcome to play out on my field' – that's before these houses were built. So off we go and we levelled a bit off and we made quite a successful cricket pitch of it.
Bill Curtis

Walter the Monster and other carnival figures outside the YMCA, Bath Road, 1931
Lyndon Davies

As the days went by and the War was over, different things happened and you had the Y.M.C.A. in Woking started, and Scouts and Cubs.

I like football and I played for a team called Woking Rovers. I also belonged to the local Y.M.C.A. in Bath Road and I used to go up there most evenings.

I loved table tennis and I did quite well at table tennis but then, in my latter years, I had to decide on table tennis or football and I chose football as what I did. I took it seriously, but I had many happy hours at Woking Y.M.C.A.. You had everything there – you had snooker, you had table tennis, you had everything. You could then get a cup of coffee or a piece of toast or anything like that. You had meetings about football, you did a bit of everything.
Philip Ledger

I had many happy hours at Woking Y.M.C.A.. You had everything there – you had snooker, you had table tennis, you had everything.

We used to go to Walton Road Mission Hall for the Girl Guides, and we used to go round there for the Young People's Union, we called it the YPU. That was a little church affair where you went in four groups. One lot would be doing needlework, one lot would be doing perhaps painting, one lot would be doing something else – four different corners and then when you went the next week you swapped round, so you all had a chance of doing the different things. That was Young People's Union. It was held one evening during the week, I expect for only an hour, that's all.
Betty Curtis

We mostly went on day trips on the train, because in those days, you used to get excursion days and it was so much more convenient just to go straight there. Because we were so near the station, we've always used trains. The thing I remember was that if you went to London shopping, if you got out and caught the 7.06 train from Woking, you got a workman's ticket.
Emily Gloster

Our summer holidays, for instance, was a train down to Devon. Stay with relatives down in Devon and back again. For two weeks normally. You get the fast train down to Exeter, Exeter St David's. Change at Exeter St David's for Torquay, where we used to go. And that was literally the old sort of 1940s, '50s style holidays.
Richard Wooller

I played hockey for the Woking Grammar School old girls, even when I was working. We used to have to work on Saturday mornings in those days, and worked till one o'clock. And I used to have to take all my hockey clobber with me and change in the office.

I was always keen on sports, so I played a lot of tennis and played hockey for the Woking Grammar School old girls, even when I was working. We used to have to work on Saturday mornings in those days, and worked till one o'clock. And I used to have to take all my hockey clobber with me and change in the office, and then I'd meet a friend came from Woking, and she worked elsewhere in Guildford and we'd probably go to Jo Lyons and have a lunch for about ninepence or a shilling. And then we'd take ourselves off to wherever we had to go to play hockey. I mean, it might have been in Guildford, it might have been at Walton-on-Thames, or it might have been Camberley, we used to go all over the place. We used to have to get ourselves there but we had quite a lot of fun.
Joan Roberts

Woking Girls Grammar School Under-15s Hockey Team, winners of the Surrey Schools Hockey Tournament, 1975 *Woking County Grammar School for Girls Magazine 1974–75*

Then we used to go swimming in the park. It was open air, it was an awful old place at the time we were children, open air you know, but we used to go.
Betty Ablett

On Sunday afternoon we all used to meet up at the swimming pool in Woking Park and just sit around and chat and push one another in. Young people showing off again round the boys!

There was a big outdoor swimming pool but you weren't allowed in there in case you got polio.
Wendy Davenport

On Sunday afternoon we all used to meet up at the swimming pool in Woking Park and just sit around and chat and push one another in. Young people showing off again round the boys! It used to be mums and dads and the kids and the likes of us youngsters just laying around and having fun.
Joyce Gee

Woking open air swimming pool, 1935 *Ann Squibb*

The swimming pool which was in the park was an open air swimming pool, built 1935. In the summer months, you spent many hours down there laying around trying to get brown. I never swam particularly well. The Grammar School used to hold the school swimming competitions there. That was a very pleasant part of the park.

I remember the golf putting course which was thru'pence – 3d that is, not 3p – where you'd go round just a short putting course and there was no driving. You just had a putter, so you could get a hole in one at every hole if you were that good, because it was just a straight putt. The park, the rest of it was very much as it is now, leading out to White Rose Lane on one end and up to where the Cotteridge was.
Anthony Dorman

There used to be a swimming pool in the middle of Woking. I suppose that was where we went. They had problems with it, because there was a hall underneath the swimming pool and the swimming pool used to leak into the hall. But I think that was where we went to swimming classes. It was really quite handy. It was in the middle of town, I suppose where the relief road is now. You had roads either side there, and it was very convenient. Office workers used to go there in the lunch-hour and have a swim.
Rosemary Christophers

There used to be a swimming pool in the middle of Woking. They had problems with it, because there was a hall underneath the swimming pool and the swimming pool used to leak into the hall.

Woking used to have a fabulous swimming pool that was knocked down. I know they built an even better one, they built the Olympic Pool, but, at the time when I first lived over this way, the swimming pool was quite lovely. It was a big pool, bigger than where I'd lived at home, but it was the fact that it was raised up high with a glass wall all the way round and it was actually on a roundabout, or traffic certainly travelled round it. I'm not sure if it was actually a roundabout as such but the traffic went round it and it had this brown, smoked glass but you were raised up and, when you were in the pool or round the edge of the pool, you could look out and see people going past in their cars and there was just something really snug about it because you were in there and it was so lovely and warm and the glass was all steamy up and yet life was going on. Traffic was all travelling past outside. It sounds, probably, very silly, but it just felt a very, very nice cosy place to be.
Elizabeth Seward

We used to spend a lot of time listening to radio, ITMA was very popular and 'In Town Tonight'. That was the evening, really, because you couldn't go out, it was blackout and sirens might go.

There was a Woking Choral Society which I joined later, in the 1930s, and Woking Music Club, which was really a subscription concert affair with celebrities coming in and playing to the members in the Woking Grammar School, which had a very lovely hall. Dinner jackets were worn before the War.
Graham Thomas

There was the Woking Music Club. I have programmes dating back to certainly the 1940s. I can't remember whether it was during the War or just after the War, but music was very important and I went to concerts.
Bernadette Rivett

I can remember of course we used to spend a lot of time listening to radio, and ITMA was very popular and 'In Town Tonight' and things like that. And that was the evening, really, because you couldn't go out, it was blackout and sirens might go; so you stayed indoors and listened to the radio.
Pat Lambert

Soon after the war when demob came about, Mr Frank Moulding came to Woking, who was a wonderful singer and he became the choir master at the Wesleyan Church and I was in the choir at that young age. About six I was there. They had a nice big choir and he was the one that reset up the Epworth Choir after the War and of course it's gone on.
Betty Ablett

Maxwell's Record and TV shop, Chertsey Road, 1973 *Philip J Moll*

The records were 78s, they were enormous, they were big 78s. There would be about six in the 'Eroica' and then eventually we got the sort of record player where you could put three on and they fell down without you having to manually change it.

Of course piano playing was the way of entertaining in those days. They would all get round the piano on a Sunday evening and have songs and everyone would do their bit as well; everyone could stand up and sing something. So it was quite common, it was the form of entertainment. It would have been before radio and miles before television.

So I bought my first classical record at Maxwell's, near Victoria Arch – there was a wonderful record shop where you could go into little booths and listen to records for ages. I had to buy some occasionally – this was later when I was obviously earning a bit. I did a paper round and the first record I bought was the 'Flying Dutchman'. It was a sailors' chorus from 'The Flying Dutchman', that was my first record and the second was the 'Eroica' Symphony. Anyway, eventually we got a record player, a proper record player.

Of course piano playing was the way of entertaining in those days. They would all get round the piano on a Sunday evening and have songs and everyone would do their bit as well; everyone could stand up and sing something.

The records were 78s, they were enormous, they were big 78s. There would be about six in the 'Eroica' and then eventually we got the sort of record player where you could put three on and they fell down without you having to manually change it. So that was a big step forward, so then you could just sit there and listen to them and they would drop down on their own and you'd only turn it halfway and then you'd go to the other side.
Barbara Beaumont

When I left school I worked for my father on the lorries. My age was put up to drive the lorry because it was the wartime era, you know. I worked with him and I used to do the band and use the lorry, and the lorry was all painted with the band on the side. I used to work from Bramley moving ammunition, taking it in the sheds, and they used to clean it, the women, and we used to take it back and put it in the sheds in the trees. It was a massive operation down at Bramley near Basingstoke. I used to play in the band at the American bases and I used to play at all the Army Camps. Then I did the Atalanta and the California England (at Wokingham) on that Sunday night. Every other Sunday at the Atalanta and every other Sunday at the California.

It was a mixture of people went to the Atalanta, lots of the people that lived around Woking. There was a lot of military people that used to come from Inkerman Barracks, particularly on Fridays and Saturdays, Inkerman Barracks at Knaphill. That's where the prison was and the CMPs were there, that was their depot.

Then, of course, I worked at the hospital, Brookwood Hospital, I used to do one Saturday a month there and then I used to work at the Bisley Shoot, there was a ballroom there. The hospital, Inkerman Barracks and the Shoot – three places and the Atalanta Ballroom.

As I got more bands I didn't do those jobs, I used to put my other bands in. We had two bands and in the end we had about six or seven bands. I used to broadcast nearly every day – Music While You Work, Workers' Playtime, early morning music and late night music. We used to put it in the can – go up and do five or six things – and they used to use them different nights in those days. The Bob Potter Broadcasting Band we used to call it.

It was a mixture of people went to the Atalanta, lots of the people that lived around Woking. There was a lot of military people that used to come from Inkerman Barracks, particularly on Fridays and Saturdays.

Atalanta Ballroom and Christ Church, Commercial Road, c.1960 *Woking History Society*

By that time the Atalanta was changing as well. We now owned it – we owned the lease of it because the lady died and the manager carried on managing it for the solicitors and then he died and I took the lease from them, and then I ran it from then on. I could see the dance band side was going, it was moving more into the groups, and then we put bingo in to make it pay as well, two nights with the bingo. In those days it was hard. The bands didn't get a lot of money and money was different then to what it is today. You could go out and have a good night out on a pound, you know, and still have change! It was ridiculous. I ran that and at the same time I took over another ballroom I was working at, the Agincourt, Camberley, I took that over as well. That was more like the Cavern in Liverpool because all the groups went there. Any group that was anything always played the Agincourt and all the big stuff from Liverpool and all the acts from America went there.

The Atalanta was an old church. And then at the side of the church was the building where the hairdressers was, and in the middle there was a garden. Now that garden, I built that garden into another club and that club was something special because you couldn't get in there until 11 o'clock at night. After 11 it would open but it would only be for musicians. So all the vehicles used to park; sometimes you would get ten, twenty of our coaches, twelve-seaters, all our bands had a twelve-seater coach or a ten-seater or something like that. They used to pull in, come in and have a meal and all sit in and play and it was like relaxing, and wherever they were playing they would head back for the Atalanta Ballroom. The ballroom would be closed and they would go to the side door, it was like all private, the public couldn't get in and we used to finish about 3 o'clock in the morning.

The bands didn't get a lot of money and money was different then to what it is today. You could go out and have a good night out on a pound, you know, and still have change! It was ridiculous.

Every night there was something on at the Atalanta Ballroom. Sunday afternoon was bingo, Sunday night was dancing. Monday night was names – group names. Tuesday night was bingo, Wednesday night was ballroom dancing. Thursday night was bingo again. Friday, dancing or groups and Saturday the same, right the way through. And then we used to do all-nighters – on Saturday night there would be an all-nighter; an act would come from Camberley and they would work there and they would get there for half past 12, 1 o'clock, 2 o'clock, 3 o'clock in the morning and we would finish at 5. That would be like Jerry Lee Lewis, Little Richard, that kind of an act, big American acts but they were too expensive to put in the Atalanta Ballroom and they would be too expensive to put in the Agincourt so what we used to do is book them for the week, two of them, and on Saturday night they'd do the Atalanta Ballroom, then they'd go across to do Agincourt and then they'd go on to do the Palais. Then the other band would go from the Palais and do it the other way round.

People wouldn't worry about noise so much then; the Atalanta never had a problem with noise, the Agincourt didn't have a problem with noise but the Palais did because it was next to people, but people used to not worry about it in the war time – just after the war and all that, everybody was out having a good time, weren't they? The price to go in the Atalanta would be half a crown, a two bob hop or half a crown and perhaps on a Saturday night five bob.

An artist came and he used to have weird ideas. He said, 'I want to paint the Atalanta' – it's all wood and everything – 'I want to paint it out like a Western scene.' I said, 'You can't do that – we have masonic dinners here on Thursday nights and Fridays.' He said, 'We'll do it like a stage set. We'll put it on a canvas, two-by-one like, and you can move them and they clip together.' That's what we done. Of course, it took the ballroom overnight and then he came to the Atalanta and he said, 'We'll do this Atlantis, under the sea.' And he painted it all out, emulsioned the whole ballroom. We had rollers and as we done it he came along and put the dayglow on and then the lights, and it was a different place altogether. When you walked in it was electric, so the whole thing came alive. It was then the 'in' place to be, and that's how we used to change it, put themes in them.
Bob Potter

'I want to paint the Atalanta' – it's all wood and everything – 'I want to paint it out like a Western scene.' I said, 'You can't do that – we have masonic dinners here.'

The Grave Diggers Skiffle Group playing at the Club Butaca, 1957.
Back (left to right) Chris Smith, Terry Crowe, Ray Stott, Trevor Dean;
Front (left to right) Nobby Besch, Lou Lewis *Trevor Dean*

THE GRAVE DIGGERS

The best music night in Woking was 1965. It was Jerry Lee Lewis' '65 comeback tour and he came in the Atalanta on a £200-a-night gig. He was just magnificent and I can remember all the girls screaming.

No one had any money, we were just working class kids. For me music was everything. Anything I could do with a guitar, I was gone. You have to remember it was rock 'n' roll. We were playing skiffle bass. This was '56.

The best music night in Woking was 1965. It was Jerry Lee Lewis' '65 comeback tour and he came in the Atalanta on a £200-a-night gig. He was just magnificent and I can remember all the girls screaming. It was great and he just walked across, stopped the band, 'Hold on boys.' He had a great accent up close, great accent, and he said to the girls, 'If you wait till the show's finished, you can all have a piece of me!' and he meant it as well! Hard drinking man.
Trevor Dean

Gigs were at the dance hall called the Atalanta and I didn't go there because that was supposed to be considered rough, so my parents wouldn't let me go there anyway. I remember probably in the early '60s seeing the teddy boys there with their quiffed hair and shirts and bovver boots, and I used to say, 'I can't go there because it's a bit rough.'
Jennifer Wharam

Every Friday night we would go to the local disco. There used to be the Woking swimming pool where the Peacocks Centre is now. It was an indoor swimming pool with a pool disco underneath. That was quite good.

Then there used to be Centre Halls. It was mainly Saturday night when everyone went. That was mainly through my teens and I used to go down the pub, then to Centre Halls disco or nightclub, it was a nightclub. That finished at two. That closed down and then there was a place called Fantails in Woking Peacocks Centre and that was good 'cause they used to have bands on from the '70s and '80s, bands that was on telly.
Derek Drake

There used to be the disco in Knaphill. That was awful. Bloody awful! And every night was a nightmare when that finished. The bus drivers! I remember one night one driver just didn't stop. There'd be a queue of people going back to Woking and he knew there was always trouble on that last bus, to get home, and he just took one look at everyone and just drove straight off. And, another time, they had a police escort. I remember that. The bus would actually have a police escort going home from Knaphill to Woking. That was in the early '70s.
Enzo Esposito

We never went to public dances until the War and then everybody did. The War changed all that sort of thing, knocked down a lot of fences, which was good.

We had dances. Brothers of our friends – and they would bring a friend at the Atalanta in Woking. That was THE dance hall. That was the tops! It wasn't very impressive. It had a sort of nice entrance and there was a little recess I think for your coats. It was all full length ballroom stuff and our friends had these dances there and we finally had our – they call it 'the coming out one.' We never went to public dances until the War and then everybody did. The War changed all that sort of thing, knocked down a lot of fences, which was good.
Katherine Buchanan

Yes, the dances, you had the Atalanta, the Labour Hall, the Woodham Church Hall, Onslow Hall in Guildford Road and Chobham Village Hall. Dancing was Saturday Special. We went to a Miss Collier to learn. She had her dancing lessons at the Labour Hall down Clarence Avenue. It's gone now.
Bill Curtis

There was a place called Fantails in Woking Peacocks Centre and that was good 'cause they used to have bands on from the '70s and '80s, bands that was on telly.

When I was seventeen there used to be dances at Brookwood Hospital. We used to cycle there and for the price of the entrance, you would get a cup of coffee and two cakes thrown in at the interval.

When I was seventeen there used to be dances at Brookwood Hospital, which was then the lunatic asylum and we used to go every fortnight. We used to cycle there and for the price of the entrance, you would get a cup of coffee and two cakes thrown in at the interval. There was a tiny little cloakroom and all the girls used to get off their bikes and steam in there because they had to get all the mud splashes off their stockings and get their hair right – headscarves were what we wore in those days – and then get yourself about presentable and get out there and stand all along one side with the boys on the other side.
Barbara Beaumont.

Usually it was a question of trying to get a dance, but it was very unusual if you managed to get to take one of them home, because they'd be off with a squaddie or something like that.

It wasn't until I was seventeen or eighteen that we started things like dancing – dancing of course was at one of the dance halls on our circuit, the Atalanta, which is where Boots shop now is. The problem with the Atalanta was, we had to vie and compete with these soldiers from Pirbright Camp for the favours of local girls and of course, they all went for uniforms and we didn't have a uniform. Usually it was a question of trying to get a dance, but it was very unusual if you managed to get to take one of them home, because they'd be off with a squaddie or something like that. The problem with the Atalanta too was that, because there was quite a lot of rivalry between the locals and the squaddies, there were very often little scuffles and those were the days when service personnel off-camp wore uniforms, and when you came out of the Atalanta, there was usually a stream of military police wandering around with their jeeps and vehicles making sure that any miscreants, anybody doing any wrong, would get arrested.
Eric Chambers

The Atalanta's floor was sprung, and another sprung floor was the Memorial Hall in St Johns here. Of course, that was put up by the Canadians in the War. 1945 that went up.
Guy Consterdine

The Atalanta used to be great in those days. They used to have a lovely springy floor. I loved jiving and us girls we used to walk in and you always knew who was going to come up and ask you, 'Can you jive with me?' Because they used to have a jive-only, and so of course your partners picked you all ready and we all used to get on the floor and jive. It used to be lovely and the whole floor used to spring up and down. It was great. We had a doorman called Percy and he was a nice man.

> **Us girls we used to walk in and you always knew who was going to come up and ask you, 'Can you jive with me?' Of course your partners picked you all ready and we all used to get on the floor and jive. It used to be lovely and the whole floor used to spring up and down.**

We always used to meet loads of people at the Ata, like New Haw boys and people from Byfleet, people from Send. It used to be fun, there was no sort of drinking. We used to pop over the Red House and I'd probably have a lemonade. I wasn't allowed to drink. My dad would have killed me in them days, come home drunk or anything.

We always had our ballerina shoes on. They were just flat black shoes, you could jive in them and dance in them and I'll never forget, I bought a beautiful black wrapover skirt. It cost the earth. It cost £4 but it was a lovely skirt and, of course, I was very slim, very slim in my young day. So I used to have this black skirt, past the knee, nothing over the knee and these black – we used to call them ballerina –

shoes and we used to wear stockings with our little belt that went round the middle, or you just went bare legged. We used to have a blouse with the old collar turned up each side and if you've seen Grease, well, that reminds me of how we used to dress and the three quarter sleeves that turn back, and having a slim figure and no mid-riff, we used to tie it up in the middle. So all these things today are what we wore back in the '50s.
Joyce Gee

> **I met my husband at the Atalanta Ballroom in Woking and quite a few people met their husbands at the Atalanta Ballroom.**

As a teenager I used to go dancing a lot. I learned where the Railway Athletic Club is now, in Woking. They had classes twice a week; we used to go there. And then they used to have the Atalanta and the old Grand which was in Commercial Road. The Atalanta was more luxurious than the other, the Grand. It had the most beautiful sprung floor, and it had a nice café, where you could get a coffee and things like that and a nice stage. Yes, it was very nice.
Peggy Goring

There was no nonsense, there was no hanky panky, it never even crossed my mind because we just didn't behave like that.

Then we used to go dancing at the barracks. The Canadians used to put on dances in the gym hall and they used to send lorries down to Woking to pick all us girls up. There was no nonsense, there was no hanky panky, it never even crossed my mind because we just didn't behave like that. We'd go up there and they'd lay on all lovely food and there'd be a lovely army band and I used to jitterbug. I won a couple of competitions you know, and we'd have a lovely time and then we'd all pile into the lorries and they'd bring us home again and so we did that on and off all during the War. So that was a really wonderful time, you know, sad as it is. I was too young to appreciate the terrible thing that was going on, but old enough to be out there enjoying myself.
Doris Moles

I met my husband at the Atalanta Ballroom in Woking and quite a few people met their husbands at the Atalanta Ballroom. It had the best sprung floor in the south of England and a live band, no taped music or cassettes or anything like that. It was a band, and there were at least eight people in the band. It was usually Bob Potter's band. We danced on Saturdays and Thursdays. I met my husband on a Thursday night, the last Thursday in November 1953 and we were married in 1956.
Muriel Green

We'd go up there and they'd lay on all lovely food and there'd be a lovely army band and I used to jitterbug.

After the War we used to go to this club once a week at the Atalanta. We'd learn how to do all the different dances, you know, like the veleta or the twostep or the military twostep, and all those. Then once a month we'd have what we called a ball, and we had to dress up and go in long dresses, and we had little cards, and with a pencil on them, and we had to sign up with a partner to have different dances.
Joan Roberts

We used to go to the picture house. There used to be three cinemas in those days. There used to be the Ritz, the Odeon and the Gaumont. It was quite a bargain to get in. About one and nine I think, in old money. You could sit in there as long as you wanted. You could sit and watch a film twice if you wanted. No one bothered checking.
David Baldwin

The Gaumont Cinema, Chertsey Road, 1950 *The Lightbox*

There was always a main feature film and then there was a second film and then there was usually a cartoon and loads of adverts. Of course, we had the news as well. It was a good programme for 1/6d wasn't it?

My favourite cinema was the Ritz in Woking. It had the organ didn't it? It was a continuous performance cinema. There was always a main feature film and then there was a second film and then there was usually a cartoon and loads of adverts. Of course, we had the news as well. It was a good programme for 1/6d wasn't it?

The organ popped up at any time between anything, I suppose when the projectionist wanted a rest! He'd play the popular things from America. He didn't go into classics or anything, it was the popular songs.

The last performance always finished with the National Anthem and that was about 10 p.m. I think, because there wasn't exactly a curfew, but you didn't stay out very late. I think it was about 10p.m. the final performance. You could see the end of the film was coming and there was a tendency for people to get up and walk out, so they didn't have to stand up for the National Anthem. But most of us sat there patiently till the end of the film, probably mopping our eyes with the last scene and then we stood, and then gathered our bits together and off we went.
Mary White

Interior of the Ritz Cinema on talent show night, 1938 *Ann Squibb*

When we were teenagers we used to go to the cinema, and we had three cinemas in Woking, the Ritz, and the Odeon, and the Plaza . The Plaza was a small one and commonly known as the flea-pit! I don't think it was, but it was just because it was a small one and not quite so sophisticated as the others.

In the Ritz you had a whole programme, you know. You had Pathé Gazette News, you had forthcoming attractions, you had a small film, and you had the major film. Then in the Ritz they had an organ, so you got an organ recital, and sometimes instead of that you might have had a band concert. I mean, I've been to Billy Cotton and his band. There were usherettes with their torches, and they had a tray of things where you could buy things in the interval sort of thing. You got a lot for your money.
Joan Roberts

And in Duke Street they had the Odeon, which was called the Astoria when it was first built and they had an organ in there. And then the oldest one, which was down further, it was an old place I must admit, and it was called the Plaza[6]. And they used to have two programmes a week, different programmes and films. But very, very old it was because I remember going there, and if you moved in the seat the whole row moved.
Peggy Goring

6 The Plaza became the Gaumont. (Ed.)

Now Woking has a superb theatre and we're considerable theatre goers. We go fifteen to twenty times a year alto-gether and we now find we go to Woking more often than to any other theatre.
Guy Consterdine

I used to play a lot of sport at school but I gave that up or it gave me up. Now I play golf and we walk. I don't know if walking is called a sport, an activity rather than a sport. I play golf at Hoebridge in Woking. You can be a mem-ber there as well but I'm not a member, I'm just Joe Public. Everybody can play now because at the public courses the prices have come down.
Jill Bowman

One of the features of Woking is the number of golf courses. If you're an enthusiast, that's really, really good and for a lot of people I know, playing golf is the object in life.
Paul Russell

I was into darts. There was a Ladies League, and we all used to go different places to play. I played there for thirty-four years in that league. I was fairly good really. Won different things, you know.
Peggy Goring

My husband was into bowls. He be-longed to Mayford Outdoors and Guild-ford Indoors. I was a bowls widow really.
Elsie Miles

The only training regime with the Woking Rovers was that you had to go and put the goal post up and the nets etc. and you didn't actually do any training, you just turned up. In those days, it was amazing, because we used to play on the Boundary Common which has now got Bellway Houses all over it, and we really enjoyed ourselves. We used to play against people in Chertsey and so forth, and Stoke Rec., that's with the Woking Rovers.

I left Woking Rovers and I then went to Woking Y.M.C.A. It was suggested that I go and have a trial at Woking and in fact, I got into the First Team and I played over a hundred games for them. Woking Town, they weren't moving with the times so much as other clubs and I think they had a big ground. Woking Football Club bought the ground for £6,000 off Woking Sports Ltd., after the War, in about 1950.

In the War the army had comman-deered the ground and they went out and left it in a hell of a state. A Mr Gosden, my father and a Mr Goddard and another two or three people got together, and they then put things together at Woking.

Walker's came in and then used the ground, and did a lot of work on the ground for us because they had a cricket ground there, where Lion Sports played cricket. They used to give the ground back to us in the winter months. The two famous cricketers from Woking, Sir Alec and Eric Bedser, used to train at Woking Football Club for hour upon hour.

In the Woking boardroom, we've got a ball 1908 and that is the ball that Woking played Bolton Wanderers with. In those days you had a lace and even in my day, you had a lace in the football, but today there's no laces, it's nice and round and smooth, but in those days you had the laces in and when you used to head a ball

it could cut your head open. Over the years, they've improved it a lot.
Philip Ledger

The only training regime with the Woking Rovers was that you had to go and put the goal post up and the nets etc. and you didn't actually do any training, you just turned up.

Phil Ledger is – was – Chairman of Woking Football Club. I played for Woking Football Club for two or three years, and had forty-four games for Woking in the old Isthmian League. We used to have to play against Oxford on a Wednesday evening or Tuesday evening, and that was before motorways. So we had two and a half, three hours trek to get there and we didn't get back home until sort of midnight, one o'clock in the morning. We also had to play at Barking, Walthamstow, Romford, Leytonstone. Again they were all up the East End of London, and that was a horrendous coach trip going there. We used to leave at ten in the morning to get there. Again, get back at ten, eleven o'clock at night.
Richard Wooller

Woking v. Bolton Wanderers at Pembroke Road, 1909. Woking lost 4-1. *The Lightbox*

I like to play football. We go to Woking Park and the Leisure Centre. We play there. We go with my cousins, play football and stuff like that and we play tennis. We go to swimming sometimes, just ladies this is. I don't go to the gym any more. I used to go. I like playing football. I support Arsenal. I'm into cricket as well.
Student

We were the kings of the road as you call it then, as cyclists, and we used to go out in cycle clubs and it was great.

I got involved in cycling. I love cycling and you could get to places that I'd never been to and of course, there was no cars on the road then. In fact I always remember coming the other way from Byfleet and there used to be thousands of people work at Vickers Armstrong at Byfleet and all the roads were covered in bikes all going one way and this one car came along and peeped its horn and there was so much abuse. But we were the kings of the road as you call it then, as cyclists, and we used to go out in cycle clubs and it was great.

I belonged to the Charlotteville at Guildford then and if the leader was up the front, and he'd be in plus fours mostly, probably a collar and tie, you were not allowed to pass him, you just sat back in the ranks, but you went to places. You went over Hindhead and down the other side, even to Portsmouth and places like this and it was cheap really. You had these little cafés and little places and you took stuff with you.
Fred Woodhouse

We all took part in the opening of the Sheerwater Athletics track. First of all, it was just old cinder, like coke sort of thing, it was rough, you know, and they ran on that. And the high jump then, you didn't have these lovely big beds to jump on, you had a little pit of sand you jumped over on and my daughters were high jumpers, you landed on this little bit of sand. Then they got the dressing rooms in there. They had a Supporters' Club, which we used to do, and Mrs Vinall, she was the girls' captain round the Athletic Club, she trained them and she made them sort of dressing rooms so the girls and the boys could be separate. We had a little tea room there. Then we all clubbed together and finally we got lights put up. We got all them lights 'cause we had a bit of a to-do with the footballers, because once we were going to put lights up, the footballers wanted to use it and we said, "If you want to use it, you help us with it, and you can only use it on the nights that we're not doing training.'

Tuesday and Thursday was training night, from six till eight and Saturday was usually a match all over the country and Sunday was training. It still is now, Tuesday and Thursday night. My daughter still goes round there with them and so instead of having to run round up on the Wheatsheaf, they came here.

Then eventually they got a better track put down and then we had to save for this tartan track. I think it was going to be about £10,000 or something and we saved, helped towards it, and we had to put so much towards it and did sort of raffles and all sorts of different things to get it going.

Then, they got like the little stand up, but I think now they put a cover on – I think they got a grant of so much from Woking and they put so much and they've

Sheerwater Athletics Track, 2006 *The Lightbox*

had the dressing rooms re-done and showers in and I think they've got a covered stand now.
Irene Oldall

My memory of my Dad is buying me some second-hand spikes. You know the barefoot runners? I was a barefoot runner before because there was no trainers. You just had plimsolls.
Sandra Thurling

We all took part in the opening of the Sheerwater Athletics track. First of all, it was just old cinder, like coke sort of thing, it was rough. And the high jump then, you didn't have these lovely big beds to jump on, you landed on this little bit of sand.

There used to be a man in Albert Drive and his son was one of the pole vaulters in the Olympics[7] and he used to have a pole vault in his garden, and do you know, he couldn't get any money and everybody clubbed together and sold things to buy him another vault stick.
Renee Illinesi

7 Brian Hooper

Well I joined an amateur dramatics society and that takes up a fair bit of my time now, because I find it quite rewarding, and it's got a good social life as well. The Woking Community Play was the history of Woking, specifically about H. G. Wells' input into Woking. H. G. Wells, in fact, only lived in Woking for about three or four years. I think that was when he wrote War of the Worlds, but Woking makes a big fuss about H. G. Wells having lived there, because he was really only living here for a very short time, but it's a good enough excuse isn't it?
Roger Thomas

There was a pageant held in 1937. I think it was probably for the hospital extension at Kettlewell. If it wasn't, it was for the Red Cross. It was held in Pyrford Court.
Mary Young

Then there's like an arcade at The Planets. Planets has got pool tables, bowling, slot machines and ladies' squash. Part of the slot machines is called Las Vegas, which is for over-eighteens. Pool is £5 an hour for a table and there's four people at a table, so me and my friends just share it between us.

And they have evenings, like Wednesdays, when it's half price for bowling, but I don't always do that, because I've got homework or something.

Sometimes I walk along the canal. Then there's Newlands Corner, I used to go there quite a lot. That's just like woodlands and big hills where you can fly kites and have picnics and things, and there's like a little burger bar. I go there with my mum and dad and brothers.
Tasmin Perrier

We used to like going out around in this area. One of our favourite places is Newlands Corner. Newlands Corner is up on the ridge of the Surrey Hills. There's beautiful views across this valley and it's a beautiful place for the kids to play. There's copses and trees they can get in, they can climb trees, they can hide. At weekends, when we had lunch, we used to say, 'We'll take the kids up Newlands,' and we took nearly all the kids in the Path. 'Okay! Ask your Mum, check your Mum' – 'cause we knew them. 'All right?' Sometimes we had fourteen in the back.
Irene Oldall

Woking has a very, very good philatelic society. I don't know how many they've got now, but at one time five of our members actually belonged to the Royal Philatelic and you've got to have a very, very good collection to belong to them, and be very knowledgeable to belong to the Royal.
Joan Roberts

There's the U3A and I've just recently joined the Woking Seniors' Club, which is just men, over the age of sixty. We meet once a month and have a lunch and usually have a very pleasant talk afterwards on varying subjects.
Peter Green

My husband calls at Bingo, he's been doing that for nearly thirty years, on a Friday evening. I do the checking and so forth, and we're on the Executive Committee, and we're life members now.

My husband calls at Bingo, he's been doing that for nearly thirty years, on a Friday evening. I do the checking and so forth, and we're on the Executive Committee, and we're life members now, because of the work we've done.

We belong to a wine circle there, because we made our home-made wine for years and years. We go to Horticultural down there, because we're judges as well on different things, you know. He judges all the fruit, vegetables, flowers and so forth, and I do the cookery and jams, and then wine we do, both of us.
Peggy Goring

I also go to Keep Fit at Goldwater Lodge on the Goldsworth Park and the girl there is extremely good. I used to go to The Vyne at Knaphill but they stopped doing it there and so I still go to Goldsworth Park.
Muriel Green

Newlands Corner is up on the ridge of the Surrey Hills. There's beautiful views across this valley and it's a beautiful place for the kids to play.

Newlands Corner, Surrey, 2006 *The Lightbox*

I shall never forget sitting in the restaurant soon after the Peacocks had been opened and a young lady came up to serve us, it was Elizabeth and I said to her, 'What do you think of Woking?' She said, 'Do you know, I'm no longer ashamed of it, I bring my friends.'

I think there is a lot more integration of our children overall. They need to have strong morals and strong identity, if they forget that they will probably lose out.

There weren't any thefts. The allotment was safe, the house was safe, your bike was safe all over town. You didn't lock up anything.

9. Pasts, Changes, Futures

Development had been patchy over the last hundred years, so there's no depth or strength of the normal sort of things you see in a town.

I was born on 20th April 1907 at No. 4 Chertsey Road, Woking. I had a lovely family. I was the youngest of six, thoroughly spoilt, and nothing went wrong except when I was seven, of course, the First World War broke out and our childhood ended, really, because on the day, on the 4th of August 1914, my eldest sister had taken my sister Kathleen and I out to tea to some friends of hers in Goldsworth Road, Woking and when we came back, War had been declared during that two or three hours we were there. Goldsworth Road was full of military, gun carriages, mules leading them and with that day, it seemed to me that we started to grow up because the War was felt soon afterwards in 1914. It wasn't the lull that it was in 1939, so here we go.

Woking, when I was a child, in my opinion, it was much better than it is now. Well I was young and happy I suppose. You'd go in all the small shops, they all knew you. You had Fairhurst, you had Miller's outfitters, and they knew you, they'd say, 'Good morning, good morning.' Well, now they haven't got a clue who you are, you're just a body walking and they're hoping you'll spend as much as you can, aren't they, nowadays?
Betty Ablett

Dad would go down to Woking on the Saturday night. He'd probably know a quarter of the people who went by.

Well Woking was a country town, a market town really. Population about forty thousand which was about right – different to what it is today, about a hundred thousand – and it was a real market town. Dad would go down to Woking on the Saturday night. The shops used to stay open till about 8pm on Saturday night and he'd walk into town – he'd probably know a quarter of the people who went by, some people he worked with or something like that. Woking used to have a good train service; a lot of people went to London to work – steam trains, dead on time. Woking itself it was a real country town.

This was part of the stockbroker belt, or so-called then, and all round here, you'll see big houses, which have all been broken up now, but in those days, there would possibly be about three or four houses within two or three acres.
Sir Alec and Eric Bedser

Woking was a country town, a market town really.

We used to meet up and walk into Woking with all our babies in their prams you know. Well, we thought we would have a cup of tea, I think, in Woolworths, but they stopped that tea bar soon as we started going. Wasn't because of us they did that! I don't think we knew where anywhere else was, you know, that served tea. The tea bar in that Woolworths, it was right over the back on the left hand side as you go in. We nattered, talked all the time, you know.
Patricia Bell

Shopping with bikes in Chertsey Road, early 1900s *Woking History Society*

**You went into the town
and there were bicycles
everywhere and you just
put them against the kerb
with your back pedal and
never locked anything
– when you went back,
it was always there.**

**1929, there were three streets, Chob-
ham Road, Chertsey Road and Commercial Road which had the Atalanta,
which was built after we arrived.**

You went into the town and there were
bicycles everywhere and you just put
them against the kerb with your back pedal and never locked anything – when you
went back, it was always there. Nobody
dreamt of it, nobody wanted it, nobody
did it – thefts were just not open knowledge I suppose. And as for other crimes

A garden fête at the home of the Hon. Mrs Gardiner, of Green Manor, 1920s
Lyndon Davies

– well there was one murder I remember in the paper, one murder one year and that was absolutely awful, the talk of the whole place.

The High Street had just shops on the one side, but more like commercial shops, like Singer sewing machine or something, not groceries and so on. There was Central Stores for groceries and the man who wrapped everything up singly in the parcels and twiddled it around and you went to pay at a kiosk and there was one lady sitting there – Martha I think it was – and she was the only one that took the money and gave you your receipt.

At the tea parties, they never called anyone by their first name. (It was just one person that she did – Lady Roll was called Dorothy in the end, but she insisted, she couldn't bear the Lady bit; anyway, that was the only one). It was always Mrs this, Mrs that. An extraordinary bit of etiquette isn't it, rather ridiculous.

There was the Co-op, they had a dividend. We were never supposed to go there, because Central Stores was the place, and then it was Pullingers, which was a bakery, and then upstairs was a little tearoom, and then there was Lucy's Café somewhere – that was down the bottom near Woolworths and the Plaza Cinema. Lucy's Café was just a little chaste thing with about four tables and afternoon tea. They didn't do coffee then in those days very much. Maybe they did – we never did. We never drank coffee. It's taken over a bit since, but tea was the thing, and Lucy's and all sorts of little places that we didn't even know much about.

Lucy's Café was just a little chaste thing with about four tables and afternoon tea. They didn't do coffee then in those days very much.

The centre of Woking now, it looks like a concrete jungle and some of the buildings that were allowed to go up are just despicable, like that tower block, which is out of place and it is ugly, it is ugly!

H.G.Wells' Martian designed by the artist Michael Condron, a gleaming office block, and the nose of a plane sculpture. Chobham Road, 2006 *Martin Bowman*

One cinema was called the fleapit. It wasn't, of course, it was perfectly alright but it was very small and we used to go and there'd be two shows a day. So we went to both of them always, to get our money's worth because you paid a half price for the second lot.

Now there was the milk cart and then it became electric and then, of course, coal was delivered by horse and cart – great big shire horses with their rough forelegs and feet. That's right, I'd forgotten that! And rag-and-bone men, they had a little jingle. And of course builders, they often had an open thing with a horse, but you see, the War stopped all that, and things had advanced hadn't they?

We had got to a boarding house in London on Queensborough Terrace, which is opposite Kensington Gardens and near Whiteleys. Mother used to go to Whiteleys because it was American owned, and we got some of the things you couldn't get anywhere else, like corn on the cob in a tin – nowhere else! – and it was called 'stewed Indian maize.' So when we came to Woking, my mother arranged with Whiteleys to phone her every Thursday morning at some certain time for the order and they delivered it on Friday. That was for a while, then we were always sent to Central Stores for any of the other oddments.

The centre of Woking now, it looks like a concrete jungle and some of the buildings that were allowed to go up are just despicable, like that tower block, which is out of place and it is ugly, it is ugly! And some of these flats look like matchboxes, hideous. Much better now, they're getting a designer. But the Council was greedy and they allowed in all sorts of things.
Katharine Buchanan

There was very little there. There were a couple of cinemas and indoor swimming pool which was in the centre of Woking then, until it leaked. So there were various local activities like the Brownies and the Scouts and ballet school and judo classes. Richard got quite involved in swimming, he went to the swimming club and life-saving club and he went to Germany and the German lads came over here in competitions. But then as they got older, it became slightly more difficult in that there wasn't anything. I suppose their school friends made their own activities, went illegally drinking in pubs and things like that, like boys do. But apart from that, there were very little activities, pastimes for them.

Now it has changed a lot, it's far busier, there's more shops, more office accommodation, so there's a lot more people around. Whether there are more activities for youngsters I don't know. Possibly because I'm no longer involved in activities for youngsters, I'm not looking for them, but the theatre is good, and the cinemas,

there are more of them. The leisure centre is quite interesting but it's a bit out of the way if you haven't got your own transport. I think that's about all.

And there's the new shopping centre. I mean when I first went to Rowley Bristow and we went from there into Woking, there were military police patrolling the town because there were lots of army barracks, like the Inkerman Barracks, but they used to patrol the town to keep the soldiers under control. So you didn't venture in there on your own. If you went with another girl, you were a bit wary – to put it mildly. That was in the late '50s, so I think there were still the two pubs there, the coffee bar, the Atalanta – which I never ventured into, never plucked up courage to go in the Atalanta Ballroom – and a church and that was about all. The library was in an old chapel and there was Robinsons, the store, and it was a grotty place really. There was nothing there.

I think Woking was a grubby, one horse place. Now it's much busier, it's much more vibrant. Yes, it's got more going for

Woking Centre Pools, now demolished *Woking History Society*

it. I think the Council, or whoever is responsible, has actually done amazing things to it, considering that it's squashed between the canal and the railway line. They haven't had much space to expand into.

Horsell has always stopped any expansion over the canal, they really don't want it, but I presume they use all Woking's facilities and they just don't want them any closer to them.

Yes, I wouldn't say it's an interesting place but it's got more attractions now. I suppose it looks like any other modern town, but it's got more going for it.
Jill Bowman

I think Woking was a grubby, one horse place. Now it's much busier, it's much more vibrant. Yes, it's got more going for it.

There was the Yorkshire Café. It was a bakery downstairs and in my teenage years, that's where we all met on Saturday morning, upstairs in the Yorkshire Café. It was very very smart and, of course, everybody rode bicycles so there were lots of bicycle sheds everywhere, places to put your bicycles, like I'd ride up from Woodham during my teenage years to have coffee with my friends at the Yorkshire Café and we all thought it was the cat's whiskers. Now Rae Bettina was a sort of upper class shop, where you didn't go in and browse because you didn't go into shops anyway to browse in those days, you went in to buy something, and all her clothes were kept sort of in wardrobes and you'd go in and she would bring out and show you what she thought would suit you. And she would often ring mother (by this time, we had a bit more money in the family) and she'd ring mother and say she'd got several

things in. I remember going there for my first ball gown. It was off the shoulder, it was what you call a large boat neck. It was a moiré silk with mauve in it and again I thought it was really the bee's knees. There was a very plush ball that we were invited to at the Atalanta. So I remember the dances in my teenage years at the Atalanta and the soldiers from Pirbright would come and so, of course, there were quite a lot of high jinks going on between the time I was fifteen and twenty I suppose.

Woking's changed so much and when you try to think about what was there, it's very difficult now to bring it back. But, of course, everybody knew everybody else and specially the shopkeepers and, of course, Robinsons was there. That came later on, but that was a great shop to go into.

I think Woking has been designed really quite superbly and I think the Centre is wonderful – the facilities for parking are very good and the entertainment, I mean the theatre is first class, London standards, I think we should be very proud. They've still retained some of the old, the High Street, it's not like it was but then I don't want it like it was, I think it's much better as it is now. And you can still see some of the old buildings there. I would like to see some recognition of the older buildings. Might be nice for Woking I think to recognise the old Sports House and the Yorkshire café, with some sort of plaque system which says, 'Here stood the Yorkshire Café' and the Sports House.
Barbara Chasemore

Woking has been designed superbly, the Centre is wonderful – the facilities for parking are very good and the theatre is first class.

'Squaddies' at Inkerman Barracks. The presence of the barracks was felt in Woking from its inception in 1895 until its closure in 1965. *The Lightbox*

There were about seven butchers of various sorts. Now, even if you include The Peacocks all you've got to find food is Sainsbury's, which is far worse that it used to be. (Sainsbury's used to be in the High Street, more or less by the Marjorie Richardson's, somewhere like that). And now you've got Sainsbury's and you've got Marks and that's your lot for food to take home and cook.

The big change, I suppose, was Gloster's, which occupied what is now County Lettings. They were a real old-fashioned sort of agricultural gardening shop. You'd get gardening stuff and the sort of place where you could get feed for your chickens if you had any and all that sort of thing. And then there was Skeet and Jeffes, which was a place where you could buy all your hardware. I remember once buying a single washer and they actually wrote out a receipt. This is the '70s obviously. Quite old-fashioned and, of course, they've moved out now.

There had been a lot of Army influence I think, but the barracks were gradually closed down. Anyway, there used to be a sign on Woking station, 'Alight here for Inkerman Barracks.' I don't know if they were closed or not by '67. You don't get the feeling of army all over the place. But once the town centre started coming, people used to come from miles for fighting on Saturday evenings. For a fight... Yes. Meet the other lot, you know? It was much worse, in many ways, much worse than it is now.

We had the Centre Pools. Under that was The Water Hole, which was a rather ill-disciplined nightclub and hot spot for entertainment. Wasn't very successful because if you build a big dance hall underneath the swimming pool it tends to leak and it did.
Richard Christophers

It was a much smaller town than it is now, I don't think we were ten thousand – God knows what we are now. One thing I do often think about is that I could, in those days, have gone into any shop – almost – in Woking and said, 'I've come out without my purse, lend me a fiver,' and they would have done. I couldn't do that anywhere now.

Well, everybody knew everybody really and you were known in almost all the shops. That's gone. It's very much more impersonal, that's because of the numbers of people. I don't know, it's just not as friendly somehow as it used to be.

Now, they built that swimming pool but who in their right minds builds a swimming pool where they built it, and who, when they built the new Peacocks centre, builds it with absolutely no communication, really, with the rest of Woking? Mind you, whoever started building Woking in the first place between a railway and a canal want their heads examined anyhow.
Margaret Eatough

Maybe the young ones like it now, maybe they like The Peacocks and they just sort of amble around in gangs. I don't know if they're impressed, I think they must be. That's what they do, they must like it down there.

There weren't any thefts. The allotment was safe, the house was safe, your bike was safe all over town. It didn't happen – amazing really to think that kids could just wander around and leave their belongings and it would still be there when you got back. You didn't lock up anything.

And you left doors wide open, all day and go out, And the windows, yes.
Wendy Davenport

There weren't any thefts. The allotment was safe, the house was safe, your bike was safe all over town. You didn't lock up anything.

The street market still survives *Martin Bowman*

Yes, I went to Christ Church and I've been a member of Christ Church ever since I came in 1938. Now everything's different – the acts of worship, and Christ Church in itself, it's not recognisable from the inside as it used to be. We had a part of it into a café and we used to have pews and choir stalls and they've all been taken out and we have chairs and carpet on the floor now and no choir stalls, no choir. I think a choir is a part of the church and I think singing is such a joyful, nice thing to sing. Although of course they have groups now, they form different groups. They have the guitars and things like that and they still have singing, but it's not as I remember singing with the robed choirs and that sort of thing.

But you have to progress don't you? If you keep grumbling about it, things are not like they used to be – they never will be will they? A generation that's coming beyond me will think exactly the same won't they, because change has to happen, but it's the big changes that have happened in my lifetime.
Emily Gloster

But you have to progress don't you? If you keep grumbling about it, things are not like they used to be – they never will be will they?

I don't like Woking as it is, because I'm old, I'm seventy-five, and I always see things now back in the '50s, what I call the golden age. No, I think the individuality has gone out of Woking, it's all the same as everywhere else, it's hustle, hustle, hustle, bustle, bustle, bustle. No, it's no good asking me that, because I really don't enjoy it. I very rarely go into Woking, I don't go in if I can help it. I'm not saying anything about the services or anything, because I have no complaints in that way. It's just me being nostalgic about the past I suppose, and I'm living in the past but then old people tend to, because they haven't really got a future if you see what I mean. You have to live in the past, it's what you do.
Pamela Green

Christ Church now finds itself part of a modern civic square *Martin Bowman*

I suppose the only thing that is almost inconceivable to someone who hasn't been here all the time is the scale of the change that's occurred in Woking. I think the thing that appals me is the abysmal standard of the architecture. Anybody, when he wants to be sensibly critical and unbiased, should just close their minds and pretend that they're entering a Midland town, shall we say, for the first time, so that they've got no preconceived ideas, and just try driving from the Six Crossroads down into Woking, as your one approach. Your second approach must be to come from Guildford and come through and under the Victoria Arch. After that you can criss-cross Woking and you think, God almighty, do people live here? And yet, you can walk a hundred and fifty yards from all this grot and it's lovely and it's an unrivalled place for exercise, for walks, for environment. You can walk for a couple of miles straight across open land. If you go to the military lands, you can almost walk from Brookwood to Camberley.

I'm really criticising the centre of Woking – what could have been done and the opportunities that have been missed and you're stuck with them for God knows how long. It's gone from quite a sort of rustic town to a big urban sprawl but it's been controlled pretty well. I think they've done as good a job as you can expect, very well, but because of the huge increase in the population, the infrastructure hasn't kept up with it and that's the difficulty.
Derek Haycroft

You can walk a hundred and fifty yards from all this grot and it's lovely, an unrivalled place for exercise, for walks, for environment.

The changing face of Woking's architecture
Martin Bowman

I think with the development in the town centre – like you've got Planets and there are quite a lot of pubs newly opened and they're quite close to us – so we do feel a bit more worried and tense, especially in the evenings, when it gets quite rowdy. Things like that. So, I mean, I notice that Woking's developed a lot in that sense. First of all it used to be quiet. It used to be a quiet area and it's becoming – it's not a city obviously, it's a town, but it's become quite developed in that sense.
Interviewee

After the War, Woking had changed.
About the time I joined up Woking had a
population of about thirty or thirty-three
thousand I suppose and it's just about tri-
pled in size now, about ninety or a hundred
thousand probably now, so all these new
places have been built, like Goldsworth
Park – that used to be Slocock's nursery
- and Sheerwater. We used to go over to
Sheerwater looking for moorhens' eggs
because it was a big swamp over there,
'till they built that estate down there.
Used to go past there at night and it was
a ghostly place because it was all marsh
and swamp there. It always seemed to be
foggy, always seemed to be low lying fog
over the place and all you could hear were
frogs croaking and it wasn't a place to be
at night on your own.

I thought Woking was the best place
in the world. I'd been to thirteen different countries during the War – all through
North Africa, West Africa, went out east
and been in some really hot climates but
I always liked coming back to Woking, it
always used to seem so lovely and green
and clean and that after being away. I
didn't want to go anywhere else.

**I'd been to thirteen different
countries during the War
– all through North Africa,
West Africa, went out east
and been in some really hot
climates but I always liked
coming back to Woking, it
always used to seem so lovely
and green and clean and that
after being away. I didn't
want to go anywhere else.**

It's far more crowded now. It used to sort of be more open spaces around the place at the time. I don't know, I suppose, looking back, I would prefer it as it was, because it was, as I say, more open, wasn't so crowded. When we first got married I had a 1929 Austin 7 and we could go down to the coast on a Sunday and back and you might meet a couple of dozen cars but that was about it. You couldn't do that today. And if you went into Woking and you wanted something at the shop, you parked your car outside the shop, you went in, got what you wanted, come out – you can't do that today. So, you know, things have changed, whether or not it's for the better, I wouldn't like to say.
Bert Hollis

Albion Square (as it was known) in about 1920… and about 1950… and in the process of redevelopment in October 2006
Martin Bowman

I think Woking is fantastic now and indeed, during my term at the Council, we started the work on the eleven-acre site which is now the Peacocks. We had a swimming pool close by, above ground, which was not a very clever thing to do because swimming pools, even below ground, leak and the one above ground, well it was like going into a shower underneath it. And one of my cherished memories is doing a lot of work with the New Victoria Theatre and the decision at the time was, how many seat theatre should we have? And we looked at all the other neighbouring theatres and they were four, five, six hundred seaters and the intention was to put in a thirteen hundred seater and there was a bit of opposition on that, but it's made so much sense because we've got a catchment area of two million that come into Woking, see Woking and it's just a wonderful place. I shall never forget sitting in the restaurant soon after the Peacocks had been opened and a young lady came up to serve us, it was Elizabeth and I said to her, 'What do you think of Woking?' She said, 'Do you know, I'm no longer ashamed of it, I bring my friends.'
Rhod Lofting

I shall never forget sitting in the restaurant soon after the Peacocks had been opened and a young lady came up to serve us, it was Elizabeth and I said to her, 'What do you think of Woking?' She said, 'Do you know, I'm no longer ashamed of it, I bring my friends.'

When we actually moved here we were, of course, part of the first wave of settlers and, what had been the countryside – the open land – was getting built over by the estates. We were one of the first wave of settlers so we couldn't really complain about that. What I do feel about Woking is that, because it's blessed with such a lot of open ground around it – heath and woodland – it has actually absorbed the new developments quite well so that, though there were thousands of new houses, the impression of open countryside, with the Common, remains. The area is still very well wooded and it's as if the people have dropped into the landscape quite nicely whereas, I think, a lot of towns of this size would seem to have been swamped by such development. It would look ugly and raw and pink and so it stayed for years to come. But you know, there are almost still secluded bits of the environment. It's possible to walk just ten minutes from here and feel that you are still in the country so I think that's very precious. You know, you would hate to think that Woking's just a convenient place to get out of. It's obviously a very good commuting town but it's also a pretty pleasant environment in itself as well as a useful and convenient place to live.
Hilary Mantel

Woking was a one-horse town he reckoned and the horse was thinking of leaving. Its development had been patchy over the last hundred years, so there's no depth or strength of the normal sort of things you see in a town.

Well, I think when I came it was probably about halfway through a process of change which had been going on since the late '60s I guess. At that time – and this is a quote from one of the councillors who was born in Woking and has lived here all of their life – in those days Woking was a one-horse town he reckoned and the horse was thinking of leaving. It was a town in the '60s which didn't have the history for it to rely on. Its development had been patchy over the last hundred years, so there's no depth or strength of the normal sort of things you see in a town.

It was then I think – as it is now – the biggest town in Surrey, population bigger than Guildford although Guildford as a whole is much larger in area. But it was punching well below its weight and the Council at that time decided that it needed more and better shopping, better roads, more people, more business and towards the end of the '60s, they decided that this was something that they wanted to initiate and by the time I arrived, a lot of that initiative had been delivered. There was more and better shopping, there were more houses and people, more business premises had been built, and a lot of the centre of the town had been redeveloped, not always to the good and there are some parts of which were quite dire, but a huge amount of change had taken place then. Since then, I think even more has taken place and it revolves around the town centre, more and better shopping, more entertainment, more public offices, more business and generally an increased level of activity and vitality in the town centre and that spread also to the villages.
Paul Russell

Hi-tech Woking *Martin Bowman*

You know, you would hate to think that Woking's just a convenient place to get out of. It's obviously a very good commuting town but it's also a pretty pleasant environment in itself as well as a useful and convenient place to live.

It's very difficult for local people to be able to afford to buy houses in the borough and it's very difficult for employers, the Borough Council included, to be able to recruit and retain staff.

The Borough Council is the only local authority in the country ever to have had a Queen's Award for Enterprise and that's for energy services. We have a very forward thinking approach to energy and environmental initiatives and there's a lot of work going on in that field at the moment and I'm involved in that, and we're doing a lot of work on the health and well-being agenda to try to improve opportunities for everybody to be able to access facilities for them to enjoy better health, not necessarily to be or become top Olympic sportsmen, but to be able to enjoy life and make the most of life.

The other big challenge that we're facing at the moment is finding ways of providing affordable housing because housing is very expensive in this area. It's very difficult for local people to be able to afford to buy houses in the borough and it's very difficult for employers, the Borough Council included, to be able to recruit and retain staff and we see this being reflected throughout many, many services, whether it's nurses, whether it's the police, whether it's the retail sector being able to recruit staff. So there's a very big problem there and we need to find innovative ways of providing some affordable housing.
Douglas Spinks

I think the challenge now is greater than before. It will be more destructive if it's not resolved, for a lot of reasons. There won't be a limit on just an area or a period. 'Paki bashing', even though it was nation-wide, was seen to be very intense but it wasn't worldwide. The problem with '9/11' is that it's worldwide and therefore it involves countries and nations that may not be party to it, being sucked into this problem.

I think there is a lot more integration of our children overall. What I see as dangers for them are that they need to have strong morals and strong identity, because I think if they forget that they will probably lose out and as a society I think we will lose out. And I don't think there's any limits to their success if they want to keep it, because Britain is changing, it's changing daily and it's changing for the better as well. I have my reservations on certain things but that isn't on the lines of being a Pakistani or being a Muslim, it's on the lines of how we as a society are going. And therefore we all have similar reservations – maybe we don't express them as much – and I think there will come a time when people will stand up and say, 'No, enough is enough, we don't want this!'
Shamas Tabrez

There are worse estates, but again there are better. We've got a nice rec. and it's nice that end, nice up the other end, but in the middle, where the shops are round here, that's where mainly all the kids seem to hang around and, you know, cause the trouble.

I hope we can get rid of most of the drugs. I mean I suppose you never get rid of them 'cause they're all over the place anyway, not just the Sheerwater estate. Make it more safer, you know.
Derek Drake

Woking needs more clothes shops.

Bigger houses.

An ice-skating rink.

To stop the vandalism as they just graf-fiti things everywhere. Yeah, they always say, 'Oh, we don't have anything to do.' And if they stop vandalising things then we'd have more money to spend on things to do. If they weren't painting all of that they could use that money for something else. Like more games stores or something like that.

More cinemas...
Bishop David Brown School students

Children with police car, 1997
Salma Sulaimani

I think there is a lot more integration of our children overall. What I see as dangers for them are that they need to have strong morals and strong identity, because I think if they forget that they will probably lose out and as a society I think we will lose out.

Index of contributions

Greta Ledger; Elsie Miles and friends; Mary Young

General index